# HIDDEN WONDERS
# OF THE HUMAN HEART

# HIDDEN WONDERS
## OF THE HUMAN HEART

## HOW TO SEE THROUGH
## YOUR SORROW

*A creative guide to revelation and renewal*

## SUSAN HOLLIDAY

Matador
9 Priory Business Park,
Wistow Road, Kibworth Beauchamp,
Leicestershire. LE8 0RX
Tel: 0116 279 2299
Email: books@troubador.co.uk
Web: www.troubador.co.uk/matador
Twitter: @matadorbooks

ISBN 9781 800464 636

British Library Cataloguing in Publication Data.
A catalogue record for this book is available from the British Library.

Cover illustration: *For the Love of Spring*, an original artwork by dee nickerson ©

Printed and bound in the UK by TJ Books LTD, Padstow, Cornwall
Typeset in 12pt Bembo by Troubador Publishing Ltd, Leicester, UK

Matador is an imprint of Troubador Publishing Ltd

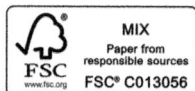

MIX
Paper from
responsible sources
FSC
www.fsc.org
FSC® C013056

In memory of Peter Holliday

*whose heart was full of wonder*

*Never has it been more urgent to speak of seeing.*

Frederick Franck – *The Zen of Seeing*[1]

# CONTENTS

Author's Note                                             i

Introduction                                             1

## PART ONE

1. The Nature of Wonder                                 13
   *Cassy's story ~ 'A crown beneath her feet'*

2. Beholding                                            28
   *Jake's story ~ 'The lost valley'*

3. A Moving Image                                       42
   *Sam's story ~ 'The garden of magical possibilities'*

4. The Hidden Face                                      58
   *Ralph's story ~ 'Totems of toughness'*

5. A Tender Vision                                      70
   *Anita's story ~ 'The nub of coldness'*

## PART TWO

6.  A Seeing Place                                              87
    *'The sealed chamber'*

7.  In the Blink of an Eye                                      96
    *Rachel's story (part one) ~ 'Caught red-handed'*

8.  Views of the Interior                                      107
    *Rachel's story (part two) ~ 'Inside the Minotaur's house'*

9.  The Language of Revelation                                 117
    *Ella's story ~ 'The shredding'*

Epilogue: The Nature of Insight                                133

About the Author                                               134
Acknowledgements                                               136
Sources                                                        140

# AUTHOR'S NOTE

*Perhaps somewhere, someplace deep inside your being,*
*you have undergone important changes while you were sad.*[2]

Rainer Maria Rilke

In the midst of change and loss we look for signs of new life. The first tender shoots often surface in the intimate spaces of our hearts, through a disturbance in our innermost thoughts and feelings.

When I first picked up the phone to make an appointment with a psychotherapist, some thirty years ago now, I wasn't heartbroken or unhinged. I wasn't the victim of catastrophic neglect or unspeakable trauma. I just knew I was lost and stuck and inexplicably sad. My heart was heavy with a kind of everyday pain, which felt baffling and unwarranted. I half expected the therapist to tell me to dry my eyes and stop wasting her time. She didn't.

What began then was a journey of discovery which has enriched my life with wonder and insight. In the conversations that took place between us, I began to understand that the ebb and flow of my feelings were not meaningless. Threaded through the needle of my suffering I discovered a hidden and deeply personal wisdom. My heart, it turns out, was trying to alert me to something extraordinary. A seed of my future self was taking root, trying to push its way through a narrow crack into the light. Caught in an old vision of myself, I was wholly unaware of this nativity.

The great German lyric poet Rilke speaks of these moments of unbidden disturbance. Writing to comfort his young friend in his sadness, he suggests that an unfamiliar presence has entered his heart. Something in him has changed, as a house that a guest has entered changes:

> *The future enters us in this way in order to be transformed in us, long before it happens. And that is why it is so important to be solitary and attentive when one is sad.*[3]

In those early months of therapy I learned to look more deeply and tenderly into my feelings. What I began to understand was this. My heart was heavy because I could not *see* the important changes that were taking place within me. Mine was a sorrow of hidden wonders, of disregarded insight, of new life overlooked.

Distracted by my busy life and ashamed of my unruly feelings, I didn't know how or where to look. In truth, I didn't even know there was anything more to be seen. Beguiled by a contemporary world view which considers sadness a disorder, a malaise, a failure of resilience, it had not occurred to me that my distress could be a kind of morning sickness. I was pregnant with seeds of possibility which longed to be revealed and realised in my life. My sadness was nothing less than the sorrow of an unseen conception. A symptom, I now understand, of a sort of blindness.

It dawned on me then. I need to learn how to see into the hidden wonders of my heart.

*

This is a book about seeing. Drawing on two decades of tender vision in my therapy practice, I want to show you ways of seeing through your sorrow, there to discover the intimate wisdom which stirs in your heart. I have chosen the word 'sorrow' because it conveys a kind of dignity of feeling, which is somehow missing in words like 'depression'. Sorrow is the guest that enters our lives to make us aware of something new within which longs to become visible, so that it can bear fruit.

Sorrowing is a creative practice which requires our wholehearted attention. Like its sound-cousins 'furrowing' and 'harrowing', it breaks open the hardened ground of our lives to make space for new seeds to take root and grow. It opens us to all that we may be by clearing a space for something that is about to happen. Unlike the now ubiquitous label 'depression', sorrow is a window not a seal. We look *through* our sorrow, not 'at it'.

In this age of distraction, we are wary of seeing through the surface of subjective life. Instead, we look *at* objects, *at* our phones and *at* our screens. We stick labels on everything, including how we feel. By these labels we recognise, but we no longer see afresh into the uncharted wonders of the human heart. Instead, preoccupied by our social media profiles, we demand to *be seen*.

If our seeing is to lead to revelation, intention is everything. Where we dig around for old ghosts and broken pieces, that's exactly what we'll find. So much of our contemporary perspective on mental health stops short in this way. We have been led to believe that the only thing we will find, if we look inside, is an irretrievably flawed childhood, a sullied soul. No wonder we are wary of embarking on the journey of revelation.

In my therapy practice I'm looking for green shoots, fresh currents, original fire. My training in depth psychology and my work with people of all ages and backgrounds have given me an unshakable faith in the reality that we are more than our history. Every moment is full of happening and everything that happens offers us the possibility of new beginning. By giving attention to all that rises in our being, we can find fresh purpose and creative energy for lives that are in a constant process of birth and renewal.

*

Rooted in eight true stories of love and loss, this is a work of intimate revelation. Each chapter illustrates a different aspect of seeing through the story of an individual's journey of personal discovery. These are tales of ordinary men and women who learn to see through their sorrow. In their own unique way, each discovers a vital intelligence that brings renewal to their lives.

The stories presented here are creative collages that allow me to portray hours of perceptive exploration in an accessible form. To preserve the anonymity of the individuals involved, I have modified events and circumstances and concealed identifying details. Where I have included a dream, this is with the kind permission of the dreamer. I have made every effort to respect confidentiality, while remaining true to the spirit of the work.

In the pages that follow, I won't dazzle you with diagnosis or blind you with jargon. To see into the wonders of the heart we need words that are warm-blooded, personal and particular. We will look beyond the two titanic terms of psychology, 'depression' and 'anxiety'. I will also be sparing with the word 'soul', although in many ways the inner quality of experience is the very subject of this book. Through excessive use, words like these risk obscuring our vision, as Rilke warns:

> One must be so careful with names anyway; it is so often the name of an offense that a life shatters upon, not the nameless and personal action itself.[4]

Despite recent progress in opening up the conversation around mental health, what happens between two people in the therapy space remains something of a mystery. 'Do you just talk?' I am sometimes asked. This is a bit like saying to a dancer 'do you just jump about?' Or asking a musician 'do you just pluck the strings?' Pressed to give an account of myself, of my life's work, I find myself drawn to speak about the art of seeing and the cultivation of insight.

Where we have understood the value of psychotherapy as a space in which we *are seen*, we may have overlooked its most fundamental contribution, as a space in which *we learn how to see*. Shielded from the glare of our everyday vision, we enter a 'seeing place'. Two by two we spend some time away from the flood. In this intimate arc of encounter we explore ways of seeing more tenderly, more particularly and more completely. This deeper vision takes us beyond diagnosis and cure. What we're after is *illumination* (to shed light on inner worlds), *revelation* (to reveal the fullness of who we are) and *inspiration* (to breathe life into dulled and desiccated selves).

At its best I believe that therapy is akin to painting, to playing an instrument, to speaking a poem or performing a play. Like these it has the potential to lift us, both seer and seen, towards a quality of vision which is equivalent to art, in that it opens us up to the richness, vitality and truth of our existence. So to explore the nature of insight, this book asks what painters, photographers, poets, sculptors and performers have to teach us about seeing deeply.

William Blake denounced the idea of the 'seer' as a person with special gifts, insisting: 'You have the same faculty as I (the visionary), only you do not trust or cultivate it. You can see what I do, if you choose.'[5] Rejecting the view that insight is a mark of genius, Blake urged the wholesale cultivation of a deeper vision, through sustained practice and faithful enquiry. Dancer and choreographer Martha Graham echoed Blake's conviction, adding 'to practice means to perform, in the face of all obstacles some act of vision, of faith, of desire.'[6] Seeing into the human heart is above all an act of vision, of faith, of desire. It involves patient enquiry, faith in the intimate truth of the moment, and a desire to unearth the incomparable nature that defines each person's being.

Along the way the practice is beset with obstacles, doubts and disappointments. In my journey as a seer I have felt more often blind than visionary. 'There are times of complete frustration, there are daily small deaths,' Martha Graham recalls. 'Then I need all the comfort that practice has stored in my memory, a tenacity of faith.' This tenacity of faith is at the heart of seeing deeply. Entering the chamber of our unseen inner spaces, we bear with our blindness until fresh insight emerges.

*

My passion for seeing has been shaped by my own creative practice as a photographer of the natural world. Before the instant snap of digital photography, I learned to deepen my seeing through the lens of my faithful Nikon camera, with its manual aperture settings and shutter speeds. I discovered that to see into the fullness and intricate particularity of a subject requires a mastery of 'depth of field'. By adjusting the aperture (opening) and shutter (closing) of my camera I can extend how far and wide I see and also in what degree of detail. The longer the aperture is open, the more I see. The quicker the shutter closes, the sharper the detail that registers.

How we open and when we close defines what and how much we see. Without a length and breadth of opening, the picture is a mere snap, lacking depth and freshness of vision. Without decisive capture, the significant moment or detail will be lost. These dynamics of perception, opening (*beholding*) and enclosing (*discernment*), also define how deeply we can see into the human heart. Opening to sustained and receptive enquiry, our attention becomes acute, until a moment of truth, or beauty, or wonder triggers a decisive moment of capture. Where seeing rushes to capture, define, or label our feelings, we fail to register the impalpable wisdom at the root of our experience. On the other hand, if we open our vision endlessly, without articulation, we get lost in what we are seeing and recoil from the flood of experience.

In the chapters that follow I will be using these doors of perception to provide a framework for our exploration into the art of seeing deeply.

- In Part One, 'The Eye of the Beholder', we explore dimensions of *opening*: How do we open our senses to take in more of the fullness and distinction of the person we behold? What part might wonder play in this opening? How can we cultivate peripheral vision, breadth of perspective and a depth of field to reveal the original treasure that lies below the surface of the ordinary human life?

- In Part Two, 'The Eye of Discernment', we turn our attention to the art of *closure*: How can we pick out the significant detail and capture the decisive moment? How does language act as an instrument of perception, to set apart a detail from within the fullness of experience and articulate it in ways that make our seeing bearable and personally meaningful?

Whilst these complementary modes are presented sequentially in this book, in reality each movement, opening and closing, circles continuously in a seamless motion.

*

During these times of global crisis and transition, we are looking for ways to replace soundbites, tick-boxes and short-sightedness with compassion, wisdom and insight. I offer this book as my contribution to a literature of hope, a growing field of writing which defies the climate of grievance and despair. We stand at a pivotal point where advances in technology are revealing to us the hidden wonders of the natural world. Perhaps the time has come for us to look afresh into the deep and vital ecology of the human heart.

Writing about his portraits in a letter to his brother Theo, Vincent Van Gogh tells of his wish to use the radiance of his colours to remind us of our true nature:

> In a picture I want to say something comforting, as music is comforting. I want to paint men and women with that something of the eternal which the halo used to symbolize. [7]

Like him, I choose to look for the best of who we are. Years of perceptive encounter have convinced me that the solace, sustenance and wisdom we seek lie not in any thing, nor in any being, but in *how we see* ourselves, each other and the living world.

# INTRODUCTION

*Joy in looking and comprehending*
*is nature's most beautiful gift.*[8]

Albert Einstein

There are times when we receive a gift which appears so slight that its true worth and significance eludes us – maybe forever, maybe just for a long time. It happened to me that hot July morning sitting in the classroom on the last day of term. We were nine or ten and our bright hearts were already turning towards the long summer break. We could barely sit still. Pens in our still small hands, we transcribed from the blackboard a single piece of homework. It went something like this:

1. Find a small patch of nature which interests you
2. With a measuring tape mark out a square
3. Make time each day to visit this square
4. Spend ten minutes really looking at it. *What do you see?*

It didn't take me long to find my square. A miniature world of lichen, woodlice and moss, crowded into the crumbling clefts and cracks of an old stone wall. Sunken deep-dappled in the shade of an ancient beech wood, the wall flanked a bygone country lane. Roots of a mighty tree lay entangled within it. Wood and stone wrapped around each other in a petrified embrace. They helped each other to stay standing. I sensed that the strength of this tender bond had something to do with the soil-swathed underworld in which the roots had their foundation. I couldn't see this other dimension, but as I traced my finger down to the toes of this ancient foot, to where the roots disappeared beneath the earth, I knew the tree didn't end there.

Years later I learned that this touching point between the seen and the unseen is known as the 'crown' of the root. This sovereign birthing place, where new life first emerges into view, has been my passion ever since.

*

My encounters that summer with this small patch of the natural world awoke in me a powerful resonance. At first I could barely endure two minutes of observation, but as the days passed the wall's dull familiarity dropped away and a beauty beyond all recognition punctured my young senses. Tiny alpine blooms in shades of dusty pink and purple mixed with a lattice of ferns and dense green clumps of moss. Each day my eyes found something new. A silver trail betrayed an early morning snail. An overnight shower saturated the stone and transformed its palette. Afternoon shade lowered the pitch. And in the cool darkness between stones, many-footed creatures busied themselves undisturbed. It was never the same square. The wall just kept on giving. Intricate and abundant. Always new.

Somewhere beyond words I began to trust in nature as a source of revelation. Wonder took root in my seeing. I let go of the idea that the wall was self-evident and began to realise that its richness was revealed to me through the quality of my looking. Over time my seeing became more sensitive to nuance, detail, trace and tone.

It wasn't just the wall that was never the same. My seeing deepened, awakened and enriched me.

This deepening of vision took place because I gave the wall my undivided attention, because in the square I had a boundaried field of vision that intensified my focus, and because I returned to see it repeatedly over time. What I couldn't have known then, and I only begin to understand now, is that this simple exercise of attending with concentration over time was to form the foundation of my creative practice as a photographer and the frame for my professional work as a psychotherapist.

In both aspects of my life I like to 'mark out a square' and ask myself *what do you see?* The square is sometimes the viewfinder of my camera, sometimes the sealed chamber of therapy. It acts like an aperture through which my seeing opens and begins to focus into a state of undivided attention. Then, like a piece of light-sensitive photographic paper, I wait, until my seeing reveals more of what is really there.

For in nature, there is always *more.*

*

Perhaps it takes the greatest of scientific minds to stand with due humility in the face of nature's unfathomable complexity, depth and intricacy. Einstein recognised that the nature which we think we see, is merely the surface of a vast and vital hinterland:

> *Nature shows us only the tail of the lion. But there is no doubt in my mind that the lion belongs with it even if he cannot reveal himself to the eye all at once because of his huge dimension.*[9]

This unfathomable realm of nature is not just 'out there' in an environment, it is also 'in here' in the depths of everyday human experience. The roots of who we are lie hidden below the surface.

These vast and vital dimensions are not merely buried in our history. They are crowning right here and now. Einstein understood that new life surfaces in response to the quality of our seeing. Sometimes it reveals itself in the slightest and most intimate of moments. At other times it roars into being.

In our rush to label and categorise those aspects of our experience that lie around us in plain view, we have perhaps lost sight of dimensions of our own nature which are budding just below the surface, at the margins of our everyday looking. To catch the tail of this lion, to reveal the full extent of our human existence, we must have faith that what lies in plain sight is not all that exists. We need to open ourselves to ways of looking rooted in an attitude of wonder.

Seeing others deeply over many years of encounter, I have been opened, enriched and touched in ways I find almost impossible to describe. Beyond the surface symptoms of troubled lives, I have discovered ecologies of feeling as intricate as coral reefs and walked in landscapes of human experience as irreplaceable as our rain forests. Yet when I tell a new acquaintance that I'm a psychotherapist, I often encounter the response 'How do you sit with all that depression?' The question never fails to floor me. It assumes that the ordinary men and women who step into my practice room are all grey, washed out and featureless, and that my seeing of them might resemble a walk through a desolate landscape on a dull winter's day. Have you any idea, I want to reply, just how much richness, intelligence and beauty surfaces from the depths of every human being, *if you just know how to look?*

*

In an age defined by its preoccupation with being seen, I find myself looking the other way. As a psychotherapist and as a photographer, what interests me is the experience of seeing. Turning my back on the shrapnel of images and sound bites that assail us, I shut my door and offer my undivided attention to another person. Don't get me wrong, I have my blind spots. Sometimes I miss what's right in front of my nose. But I try to cultivate a depth of seeing which takes me closer to the original nature that is crowning in the present moment. I look below the surface, between the lines, out towards the further margins of experience. This seeing into the human heart is fundamentally relational. It takes place in the space between us. The experience is intimate and powerful. So powerful, that it invariably transforms both of us.

Within the sheltered arc of my therapy practice it becomes possible to see more of the incomparable nature that lies in the deeper chambers of the human heart. For some, the very word 'deep' conjures up a lifeless ocean trench, a place of no return beyond the reach of light. Others imagine a dismal shadowland, heaving with hideously deformed creatures of the night. In recent times we have given this unseen dimension of human experience a fearful name. The 'unconscious'. Then, to keep the deep safely out of sight, we have invested countless millions in a way of life laced with distraction. Dazzled by larger-than-life drama, we cease to see beyond the surface of experience. Our essential nature registers as ubiquitous, bland and empty. Overlooked like our oceans, these vital depths become dumping grounds for our toxic waste.

So here's the thing. Human nature is not self-evident. Like the entangled tree of my childhood awakening, our lived experience is half hidden. It has an unseen dimension which is the fulcrum of all life. In our depths lie the nursery grounds of being, where seeds of possibility wait to be quickened into life through the warmth of our attention. Unwatered by wonder and curiosity, the very source of our aliveness risks drying up. This desiccation erodes not only the experience of those who are unseen. It also withers our experience as people who see.

Eyes trained on celebrity, we have become blind to the sovereign nature which animates ordinary human life. Unseen, our lives seem unremarkable, commonplace, featureless. We look away perhaps, for fear of discovering an interior wasteland. Our disregard reveals that we have lost faith in the existence of a wellspring at the heart of human experience, a source of emotional nourishment and personal truth that is alive moment to moment, in all of us.

In an age of swipes and clicks, our seeing risks becoming shallow and blinkered. We believe we can fathom each other in an instant. Seen through this cursory vision, human nature itself becomes distant and generic. The language of popular psychology may be contributing to the problem. Two monolithic descriptors dominate our public discourse about suffering. 'Anxiety' and 'Depression'. Like giant trawler nets, these labels sweep through the delicate ecology of the heart, lumping together the fine-grained particularity of our experience.

Ubiquitous diagnostic markers like these risk becoming cataracts that cloud our view of a complex and vital intelligence which seeks expression through our lives. Statistics published by the World Health Organization suggest that more than three hundred million people are now 'living with depression'. Presented in this way, the extraordinary diversity, subtlety and complexity of human experience become blurred into a homogenous 'epidemic'. This is good news for the pharmaceutical industry. The global antidepressant drugs market is expected to reach $15.88 billion by 2025.[10]

Disconnected from the vital intelligence of our hearts we look to things, mountains of things, to replenish the void in our being. We plunder the natural world around us to fill the bottomless pit within.

Our myopia, it seems, is costing us the earth.

*

Men and women from all walks of life are finding their way to therapy. What many of them seem to share is an experience of being simultaneously flooded and empty. Spellbound by the fear of missing out (FOMO) we try to take it all in – the tide of images, data, information, news. To protect ourselves from this inundation we dare not open deeply. Instead, we take thousands of shallow sips, grazing the surface of life. Starved of the nourishment of a more profound acquaintance, we rely on a drip feed of attention.

We are all too familiar with images of deserts and urban sprawl claiming our once abundant wilderness spaces, with the impoverishment of biodiversity and the dangers of flooding from rising sea levels. Perhaps we are not yet awake to the equivalent despoiling of our human ecology.

As a psychotherapist responding to these experiences of inundation and desolation, I find myself returning to three fundamental questions:

1. how can we restore intimate connection?
2. how can we find a sustainable source of emotional replenishment?
3. how can we cherish and protect the incomparable worth of the ordinary human life?

Perhaps we can find some answers by cultivating a deeper vision of human nature.

In the hush of pandemic lockdown we have begun to look once more at nature. Untethered from our habitual preoccupations, social media has burst forth with intimate pictures of the living world. The uncurling of a leaf. Recordings of birdsong. Buds blossoming. Abducted into confinement and severed from our surface distractions, many of us have also started to look at ourselves and at each other more deeply. We have discovered that below the surface there are hidden dramas, untended longings, pathways to undiscovered dimensions. Perhaps, we dare to wonder, there could be more to human nature than meets the eye.

At the heart of this book lies the conviction that there is no such thing as an ordinary human life. There is only the unseen life. Against the backdrop of a culture preoccupied with being seen, I want to suggest that our journey to maturity, as individuals and as a community of beings, rests in our developing ways of seeing into the deeper reaches of human experience. Seeing into the hidden wonders of our hearts, we receive a threefold blessing:

- We recover dimensions of experience that are *vital*: Connected to instincts, intuitions and dreams, the ordinary life becomes vivid and resonant.
- We encounter all that is *deep-rooted*: We discover that our roots are inextricably interlinked and remember what we thirst for most profoundly. Communion.
- We learn to confront matters that are of *grave* importance: we take responsibility for the challenges within and around us.

Beyond the surface, we discover that each of us is incomparable. Not a kind of person, but one of a kind. At the same time, this radical seeing rekindles an experience of kinship, a recognition in the face of difference of a common root. Beholding one another in our distinction and our kinship we re-ignite a desire to cherish and tend the garden of our human commonwealth, to take our place in a wider ecology of being.

It seems so clear to me now, as I reflect on my childhood experience of seeing the wall. I visited a small square of nature for a few minutes each day and asked the question 'what do you see?' I came to know this unremarkable wall intimately, in its abundant and ever-changing beauty. Wonder took root in my seeing. I found myself caring about it. A wall. How much more might we cherish the person we come to know through seeing them deeply.

# PART ONE

# THE EYE OF THE BEHOLDER

*Beholding:*
*from Old English bi = thoroughly + halden = to hold*

To open to someone (or something) with an attitude of wonder,
to comprehend the full extent of their irreplaceable distinction
through sustained attention and tender enquiry.

# CHAPTER ONE

# THE NATURE OF WONDER

*Cassy's Story ~ 'A Crown Beneath Her Feet'*

*If we had a keen vision and feeling of all ordinary human life, it would be like hearing the grass grow and the squirrel's heart beat, and we should die of that roar which lies on the other side of silence.*[11]

George Eliot

Clods of hair frame her still swollen face. Raging from the assault of last year's chemo, Cassy's new crop sprawls in tightly fisted curls, abjectly refusing to resume its once civilized composure. This shock of hair seems at odds with the rest of her diminutive frame, which looks neat and buttoned up as ever. It's been over a year since I last saw Cassy. I first encountered her in the wake of her son's departure to study at university. Surprised then by an aching loneliness, she had begun to question her life and its meaning beyond motherhood. Six months into our work, a cancer diagnosis brought these first sessions to an abrupt end.

Back now in the familiar space of my practice room, Cassy looks around, taking in the impossible fact that nothing has changed. The pot plant still stands on the windowsill. A pair of dark red cushions huddle on the sofa. The windswept seascape still stretches out its wide horizon on the opposite wall. Since she was last here Cassy has been prodded and poked, investigated, injected and dissected.

She has been wired up, filled up and drained out. Ultimately, she has been saved. Last week's scan results have given her the all-clear. Everyone is glad, relieved, grateful. With sympathetic eyes they tell her life will now begin to get back to normal.

Cassy will not look at me. A pregnant silence circles us both. I wonder if she is struggling to be seen in her altered state, mortified by the evidence of her suffering. Eventually, searching for connection I say brightly 'You've had your scan results.' In a single motion Cassy's back straightens, her head turns and she looks straight at me. That's when I realise she is feeling neither mortified nor grateful. Her look is white hot and merciless. It seems to say, 'If you so much as think of telling me my life will now get back to normal, I will take you apart.'

All at once I find myself in the presence of something unknown and very powerful. The hairs on the back of my neck stand up. Deep in the pit of my stomach something stirs. Low and prolonged, it's the kind of sub-audible sound a cat makes when it senses danger. Cassy's presence feels both intimate and profoundly 'other'. The pitiless horror of what she has been through since we last met has burned away her compliance. The notion of anything being normal again registers as an affront. Layers of cultural conditioning have been torched. The good wife, the loyal mother, the conscientious client, have all gone. What remains is a force of nature.

Cassy is ablaze.

In this heightened moment it is tempting to disarm the force of the encounter with interpretation, to rescue us both from the unspoken and the unspeakable by filling the space with words. Instead I hold her gaze. Scorched by the heat of her, I am in the presence of something entirely unforeseen. Separate and self-willed. Wild. I don't know what I am looking at. More accurately, I no longer know *who is looking at me*.

\*

Jewish philosopher Emmanuel Levinas reminds us that in front of a living face, we become aware of 'the eyes that look at you'.[12] Encountered in close proximity, the face is not primarily a physical or aesthetic object, but a 'living presence' that is wholly resistant to finite encapsulation or recognition. Through the intimacy of eye-to-eye contact, we encounter 'the epiphany of the face'.[13]

Levinas' lifelong preoccupation with the ethical importance of seeing one another face to face at close quarters draws on his witness to the effacement of Jewish people in the Holocaust. His father and brothers, along with other family members, died in the faceless butchery of the concentration camps. Levinas understood from bitter experience that the further away we stand in relation to the human face, the easier it becomes to defile, to diminish, to discount.

In the unguarded face we encounter not only the vulnerability of the other, but also something of the person's distinction, their sovereign unfathomable mystery. We see beyond the victim, the patient, the wounded soul, into an original nature that is revealed all at once, in the lived moment between us:

*The skin of the face is that which stays most naked, most destitute.*
*It is the most naked, though with a decent nudity.*[14]

Perhaps in this age of exposure we no longer trust ourselves to encounter this nakedness. Clinging to our umbilical digital feeds, we drink from an impersonal source. Flat screen glances skirt across our line of sight without penetrating. There is no opening, no taking in the living presence of otherness. Without intimate acquaintance, our perception becomes oblique and shallow. We are not much *touched* by one another.

\*

Born in small town New South Wales, Cassy set off on her walkabout at nineteen, as so many young Australians do. She looked forward to studying marine biology on her return. A wild and glorious night with new-found friends on a beach in Thailand changed everything. The unplanned pregnancy that followed turned her world upside down. Cassy chose to keep the baby. She moved to the UK with the little boy's father, a talented young entrepreneur. Uprooted from her native soil and eclipsed by his successes, she immersed herself in the realisation of his dreams. Twenty years passed. Cassy's unlived life slumbered fitfully below the surface. Until now.

Looking into Cassy's eyes in this moment I'm aware of the deep darkness of her pupils. Beyond their glossy surface, her eyes feel alive with presence. In the embers of her tamed and polished life, something vital is pushing through. At her most desecrated, she finds herself in possession of an imperative so fierce that it will clear everything in its way. This force is not blind or primitive. Fire-forged, it is alight with purpose and a raging hunger for life.

Tragically, it is often through confrontation with loss that we come to realise the depth of our responsibility to life. Cassy may have been given the all-clear from the ruthless cancer, but the life she led before her diagnosis has died. The self-effacement and acquiescence that characterised her former existence now lies in ashes. Unravelled, she stands naked in front of a ravaging truth. Her life is precious. Not because it is accomplished or worthy. It is precious because it is a one-off. Her life is irreplaceable.

Dancer and choreographer Martha Graham speaks of this singularity of being:

> *There is a vitality, a life force, an energy, a quickening that is translated through you into action, and because there is only one of you in all time, this expression is unique. And if you block it, it will never exist through any other medium and be lost. The world will not have it.*[15]

Confronted with sorrow, we are perhaps overly preoccupied with searching for old ghosts. Eyes trained on past tragedy, we miss new life budding in this very instant. These ordinary miracles flit into view in the briefest of moments and disappear as quickly where there are no arms to catch them. If I block this quickening in Cassy through interpretation or rescue, through definition, deflection or denial, 'the world will not have it'. My responsibility to this nativity is simply this: to allow the moment to swell, so that it reaches its own crowning point. Only then will the burden of its truth be released.

Dark storm clouds gather in Cassy's eyes. After some time, breaking the silence, she says with raw simplicity, 'I feel scarred beyond all recognition.' Seared by the unbidden truth of these few spare words, the heat in her bursts. Tears fall, slowly, like the first heavy drops of rain breaking a long spell of hot weather.

The poignancy of the moment is palpable. Cassy is a stranger to herself, and to me. We are both bewildered. Dislocated. Lost. Somewhere in the unspoken moment between us we both know that she has chosen to surrender to this uncharted state. Turning her back on the waymarked path that could return her to the citadel of her former life, she has wandered into the heart of her own wilderness.

Over the days that follow this encounter, Cassy's words of devastation ring in my ears. Then it comes to me. Rooting through a pile of newspapers, I find it. A recent article which describes the impact of bushfires on the landscape of Cassy's native New South Wales. Below it, an image with a caption which reads 'Acres of Eucalyptus trees charred *beyond all recognition*'. Eucalyptus, the article explains, have evolved over millennia to live through fire. In fact the trees depend on fire to some degree for regeneration. Where leaves and branches may be laid waste above ground, the tree is renewed from underground *lignotubers*. These woody swellings in the root system contain a mass of buds and food reserves, which are quickened into life through contact with fire.

In our next session, I share the image of the eucalyptus with Cassy. It's familiar to her of course. She grew up surrounded by this cycle of destruction and renewal. Standing in the light of this image, we both know that whatever new life may have been ignited by Cassy's cancer, it will surface from the deep.

In the weeks that follow, Cassy and I roam the great plains of her heart together. In this walkabout we have nothing but the songlines of her fire-forged will to guide us. All we can do is watch and wait. We wait for the new life to ripen in the darkness.

There is an intensity to this surrender. For it is precisely when we are lost that we become most fully present. Untethered from signposts, charts and familiar landmarks, wits sharpen, instincts stir, senses begin to sniff for the scent of new horizons. In this moment we don't even know what we are looking for. We just know it will not lie on the old path.

Our first glimpse of new shoots appears in a dream:

*I find myself suspended in mid-air. I'm dancing, but my feet don't touch the ground. My whole being is glowing. I am whole and unbroken. All around me I can see fields and woods, rivers and lakes. It is early morning and everything is singing. Below me I become aware of a young man. He is dark skinned, with jet black hair and strong arms. His presence is calm and sure-footed. 'I can teach you how to dance' he tells me. That's ridiculous, I think, I am dancing. Gently he persists; 'I can show you some new steps.' The thought of losing my free and weightless state fills me with panic. Imagine how clumsy I would seem on the ground. But something about the man is quietly insistent. Reaching down to the warm earth at his feet, he lifts up a braided garland and offers it to me. The crown is woven from tresses of golden hair. My hair. All at once I know that I will come down to earth. I will let him teach me. Risking everything, I will begin again.*

The dream is a gift. It tenders a vision from a place deep within her, from the roots of her being. The darkness of the man suggests that he originates in an unseen place. Surfacing from a realm of initiation, he articulates the choice she faces in the aftermath of the cancer that has ravaged her former existence. She can go back to living a provisional life, her potential suspended in the amniotic warmth of possibility. Or she can make the difficult descent, begin the journey of realising her true worth in the gravity of time and space. Knowing the path ahead will not be easy, Cassy it seems has chosen birth. Her dream is a vision of conception.

Witness to revelation, Cassy and I sit for a moment in stunned silence. Suddenly I feel very small. My sense of self-importance dissolves. It is a sweet diminishment. A remembering, perhaps. Concealed beyond anything I might assume, or think, or know, there are greater forces at play. These nascent powers are rendered in Cassy's dream with a precision and beauty that takes my breath away.

After a long silence I venture to ask Cassy how the dream makes her feel. 'Alive,' she replies. 'Free. Hopeful.' Her hand moves to cover her mouth as the pain of this lost state surges up through her throat. 'And when was the last time you felt like that?' I ask. We both know the answer. Since her unplanned pregnancy on that hope-filled journey of initiation into adult life, Cassy's dreams have been on hold. Supporting her husband's career and tending to the needs of her children, she has kicked the can of her own life down the road. Others have taken centre stage. The deep shame of having been left behind keeps her life's potential locked in suspended animation.

Like a felled tree which sprouts new shoots from the crown of its roots:

*A soul that is ruined in the bud will frequently return to the springtime of its beginnings and its promise-filled childhood, as though it could discover new hopes there and retie the broken threads of life.*[16]

Cassy's dream offers her a second chance to bloom. The garland of hair seems to represent the broken threads of life. In the dream they are re-woven. Whole. Sovereign. This detail is all the more poignant because of the devastation of losing her own crown of hair to the brutal scorching of chemotherapy. The crown represents all that is indigenous, potent and particular in Cassy's being. It points to all that is of greatest worth within her, to root values which may have become lost in the undergrowth of other people's dreams.

Like everything else in nature, each human life seeks at all costs to be wholly itself. The Greeks used the word *kharaktér* to represent this sovereign nature. Their word, which gives rise to our word 'character', originally referred to an engraved mark, made by a pointed stake or *kharax*. In nature, this indelible imprint is pregnant with potential and self-willed purpose. We all have a birthmark like this within us. It is what distinguishes each of us from all others. This imprint cannot be erased, broken, or stolen. It can however get lost, distorted, or overlaid. Through its brutal defoliation, Cassy's cancer has exposed the original markings at the core of her being. Together we face the task of decoding these markings.

To explore her original nature, I suggest to Cassy that we look back at her childhood. How did she spend her time, when time was hers to spend? Cassy arrives the following week with a bundle of childhood photographs. The youngest of four children, she was the only girl. 'I felt overshadowed by my brothers from the very beginning,' she reflects. 'Everything they did seemed magical to me. I tried my hardest to be like them. I was just grateful whenever they allowed me to tag along. It never occurred to me that I could be someone in my own right.'

I ask Cassy if there is a photograph that represents the person she is 'in her own right'. Without hesitation she picks out one of the earliest images. She is perhaps five years old. Hair wild and tangled in the salt of a sea breeze, she is sitting on a rock. Beyond her the wild Pacific Ocean heaves its might and a vast horizon dwarfs the rugged coastline. Looking directly at the camera she holds up a large crab in her tiny hand. Her eyes are fierce with joy. 'That's me,' Cassy tells me quietly now. 'That's who I am.'

It takes many more weeks for us to re-trace the steps that take Cassy back to the woman she most essentially is. The more she looks, the more she sees. She begins to recognise her original nature in all its untamed passion and unmanifest distinction. Feeling the ground beneath her feet, Cassy begins to reconnect to what matters to her most deeply. She realises that her self-effacement is rooted in a fundamental sense of insignificance in the shadow of the men in her life. She has always felt beholden, first to her brothers and later to her husband, the young man who stood by her in her pregnancy. Indebted to him, she has quite simply handed over the reins of her life to his keeping. As his career blossomed, she has followed him into ever more polished circles of success. The sea salt has been left behind.

As she reconnects to her original nature, Cassy begins to see through the ravaging of her cancer to an earlier loss of self. The full extent of this alienation is hard to bear. In time her rage yields to a deep and necessary grief. Opening herself to this process of sorrowing, she begins to make space in her life for the seeds of new beginnings.

A year after her dream, Cassy tells me that she and her husband are moving out of London. This time he is following in her footsteps. They have bought a house on the outskirts of Portsmouth. 'We want to be near the sea,' she explains. Picking up her original passion for the natural world, Cassy has enrolled on a course in Land and Wildlife Conservation at nearby Sparsholt College. The move will not be easy. There are sacrifices to be made, risks to be taken. She will study alongside students half her age. 'A part of me feels ridiculous,' she confesses. Cassy smiles. We both know from the dream that her hunger for life is stronger than her fear of foolishness.

That Christmas I receive a simple home-made card. Written in her clear hand, Cassy quotes Sioux medicine man Black Elk:

> *It may be that some little root of the sacred tree still lives. Nourish it*
> *then, that it may leaf and bloom and fill with singing birds.*[17]

*

In her much-loved novel *Middlemarch*, George Eliot makes a plea for us to cultivate 'a keen vision and feeling of all ordinary human life'. Seeing deeply into the heart of human nature, she suggests, we encounter a realm both fragile and majestic, in which the grass, the squirrel, and the lion are our kin. The more we can see into the wisdom of our hearts, the more we begin to trust that we are all held in a life-giving nature which manifests not beyond us, but through us and between us.

At a distance the inhabitants of *Middlemarch* seem to lead ordinary lives. Eliot shows us that there is no such thing. Seen deeply, each character stands out in their irreplaceable distinction. This acuteness of vision relies fundamentally on a sensitivity in the beholder, a willingness to be vulnerable to subtle frequencies, to marginal details, fine lines and faint traces. Keen vision, it seems, pierces the heart of the beholder.

We tend to imagine the act of seeing as an outward movement in which our sight travels to engage with a subject 'out there', at a distance. In my experience, seeing someone deeply is primarily an act of 'taking in'. There needs to be an opening in me. Awake to wonder, I become vulnerable to something unforeseen which cuts through the heart of my preconceptions. Perhaps this is why the word 'wonder' shares its root with the German *Wunde*, meaning 'wound'.

Troubled souls enter my therapy room like comets bearing seeds from the other side of the solar system. At first, they can appear quite broken by their long journey to this shore. It's easy to view these apparitions as harbingers of doom. I choose to remember that many moons ago comets fell on aboriginal earth, bearing in their icy rocks the chemical precursors to life. As a therapist I am rather like this aboriginal earth. My clients impact me with their pain. Yes. But they also touch me with their courage, tenderness and wisdom. They seed me with their irreplaceable presence.

Francis Bacon calls wonder 'broken knowledge'. Unburdened by preconception our senses awaken to all that is budding, fledgling, sprouting and swelling within and between us, moment to moment. We encounter an incomplete picture, a trace, a hunch, a riddle, a distant call. These dimensions of experience have yet to be bottled or labelled. Through keen vision we fathom, distinguish and understand, but we have first to bear with blindness.

This wondering stance is beautifully illustrated in the film *Tawai – A Voice from the Forest*, which documents the way of life of one of our last remaining hunter-gatherer societies. The Penan people still rely entirely on the ancient forests of Borneo for their everyday survival. In the film, we see a single figure immersed in a forest alive with colour, texture and sound. Blow pipe at the ready, he is profoundly present to the slightest movement in the canopy above. His attention is rooted in respect for the emergent and self-willed (wild) nature around him. He knows the forest intimately. At the same time, he appreciates that *he does not know the next moment within it*. As a psychotherapist I share this deep respect for the unforeseen.

In our fear of encountering the unknown, we pad our vision with preconception. Even 'the quickest of us walk about well wadded with stupidity',[18] Eliot laments. Seeing with the naked eye, we risk encountering inconvenient truths, bone-shaking burials and blinding revelations. Like the Greek Cassandra, we may find that it is not easy to bear the gift of sight in a blind and blinkered world. Small wonder then that Eliot's word 'keen' is linked to the old German *kühn* meaning 'bold' or 'courageous'.

The roots of 'keen' vision are also entangled with the old English *cēne*, meaning 'wise'. Rooted in *weid*, meaning both 'to see' and 'to know', this is not the kind of wisdom bestowed on a sage few, but the keen 'wit' which punctures our senses when we attend to something afresh.

When new life surfaces in the therapy relationship, it has a pure pitch. Like the first birdsong at dawn. No matter how many times I might have heard this sound, it still feels surprising, original and deeply affecting. There is no one-way Lazarus miracle here. As Jung reminds us:

> *The meeting of two personalities is like the contact of two chemical substances; if there is any reaction, both are transformed.*[19]

Perhaps wonder seems counter to the objectivity of science, which has so enhanced the authority of psychotherapy in recent decades. For me wonder and objectivity are not opposites. As a photographer I see into the depths of nature using the science and technology of cameras and lenses, but my vision relies primarily on the quality of attention through the eye which is alive to wonder. In the same way the tools of psychotherapy – developmental psychology, attachment theory, object relations, neuroscience – offer invaluable conceptual tools through which to view our human experience. But these concepts are just that. Concepts. They are the tools not the master. The lenses not the eye.

As a psychotherapist, I feel a kinship with photographer Bill Brandt when he confesses:

> *Most photographers would feel a certain embarrassment in admitting publicly that they carried within them a sense of wonder, yet without it they would not produce the work they do.*[20]

\*

In the century since Freud and others helped us to understand how early patterns of *nurture* shape future life experience, we have perhaps lost sight of the purposeful intelligence of our originating *nature*. In Freud's anatomy of the psyche, nature is consigned to a dimly lit unconscious realm, a dark forest seething with primordial instincts and untamed urges. At the heart of his model lies the notion of a conflict between civilised 'mind' and a state of nature dominated by primitive drives that lead us towards 'incest, cannibalism and lust for killing.'[21] Influenced perhaps by the conquering ideals of nineteenth-century explorers and missionaries who set out to subdue and civilise a 'savage' nature, Freud proposed:

> ... the principle task of civilisation, its actual raison d'être, is to defend us against nature.[22]

As though to reinforce this opposition between a civilized human and a native one, Freud abandoned a vocabulary of experience rooted in imagery drawn from our relationship with nature. He replaced it with a lexicon of abstract nouns. Words he popularised (id, ego, superego, libido) have since become ingrained in popular culture and professional practice. Consigned to a primitive unconscious, the interior spaces of human nature appear to us, as the forests of the Congo did to nineteenth-century explorers and writers, as a 'heart of darkness'. We dare not enter. Instead, we live at the perimeter where nature is levelled and enclosed. Titled and tilled – but largely untold.

Robbed of the nuanced poetic vocabulary of our native tongue, the impressions of our inner life clog together in an undifferentiated mass, a hairball of raw sensation that threatens to clog up the flow of experience. These sensations register like blind creatures flailing in a dark cave. Medicating our unruly symptoms into an uneasy slumber, we shoot the messenger. In time our organs of perception, like muscles, begin to weaken through disuse. We begin to apprehend our inner and outer worlds with a kind of attention deficit.

As we lose faith in the underlying richness of sheer being, our lives begin to resemble the depleted soil, the eroded rivers, the factory farmed fields. To find the equivalence of human depression we have only to imagine a flat plane of industrial scale single-hue rapeseed, where once lay a mixed flower meadow edged by native woodland. In both cases what is being lost is immeasurable.

In her passionate defence of the natural world and its untamed people, Jay Griffiths quotes Native American civil rights leader, Luther Standing Bear, who testified that before the coming of the white man, with his sights set on the conquest of nature:

> There was no such thing as emptiness in the world. Even in the sky there were no vacant places. Everywhere there was life, visible and invisible.[23]

The void, it seems, is a modern concept, the desolate child of poor acquaintance, born of shallow vision. Nature, be this in the jungles of the Amazon or the forest of human experience, is not a 'heart of darkness'. It is not unconscious, like a drunkard, an idiot, or a brute. Nature is more conscious than we can begin to imagine. Our suffering heart has its own necessity, which can seem obscure, but its movements are not primitive, rudimentary or meaningless. Our emotions cannot be reduced to a diagnostic table, for they give voice to a human nature that is continuously birthing and renewing and bearing fruit. Our longings, dreams and intuitions are all messages from this original realm which seeks to emerge out of its implicate state, so that it can mature and bear fruit in our lives. Jung understood this when he wrote 'Entering yourself through dreams, is touching nature from the inside.'[24]

Understood in this way emotional intelligence is not simply the application of reason to chaotic drives and random passions. It is the originating impulse itself, a sovereign reality that is 'continuous, multiple, simultaneous, complex, abundant and partly visible.'[25] This nature cannot reveal itself to the eye all at once. Catching hold of the lion's tail, we need courage and patience to see its full extent. Seeing deeply in this way, we light a fire. There is an ignition of love and will, which could change everything. As Iain McGilchrist reminds us in his seminal book on perception:

> ... the kind of attention we pay actually alters the world: we are literally, partners in creation.[26]

# CHAPTER TWO

# BEHOLDING

*Jake's Story ~ 'The Lost Valley'*

*It is part of the photographer's job to see more intensely than most people do. He must have and keep in him something of the receptiveness of the child who looks at the world for the first time or of the traveller who enters a strange country.*[27]

Bill Brandt

I am walking up the valley. Ahead of me lie the brooding peaks of the Langdale Pikes, at the heart of the Cumbrian mountains. All around the sound of water fills the air. Streams tumble down the steep slopes like children giddy with the thrill of gravity. At the bottom of the valley the waters meet. A shimmering silver ribbon marks the place where two great masses of land touch. Here the moving moment meets the stillness of all that has been before. We are all, each one of us, like this valley. An ancient landscape meeting a moment of becoming. A place where past and present meet.

It's been two hours since I left the village below. I have a long walk ahead of me. Enfolded and turned under, I am a detail woven into the fabric of this intimate place. A light rain begins to fall. Softly. In this moment if you were to offer me a helicopter ride to the summit, I would not take it. For with every step I can feel my senses opening. The tired accumulations of thought and image are being washed away like dust in the rain. Each move forward stretches the experience of seeing in time, lapping layer upon layer of impression, like paint on the canvas of my being. What I see becomes saturated, alive and particular. I begin to remember what it feels like to see with a naked eye.

Walking in nature, I have learned the first principal of perceptive insight: To see afresh, our vision needs to be undressed by time. Through gradual acquaintance, our preconceptions fall to the floor, as though removed by an invisible lover. Unclad, our eyes begin to see beyond recognition. We become 'the child who looks at the world for the first time… the traveller who enters a strange country.'

In her book *The Living Mountain*, Scottish nature writer and poet Anna (Nan) Shepherd reflects on the effect of seeing through time. Walking for hours, sometimes days, in the Cairngorm mountains, she notices how gradually her perception deepens so that:

> *The eye sees what it didn't see before, or sees in a new way what it had already seen. So the ear, the other senses [...] These moments come unpredictably, yet governed, it would seem, by a law whose working is dimly understood.*[28]

This strikes me as a beautiful description of seeing through gradual acquaintance. We see what we 'didn't see before' and we see 'in a new way'.

Rooted in the Latin *gradus*, meaning 'step', the word 'gradual' refers to something coming into fullness over time, step by step. So walking is a natural metaphor for the art of perceptive vision. In search of insight, we leave the shores of the familiar and travel into 'a strange country', hoping to return with a deeper vision to the land of more familiar forms.

\*

The practice of drawing also teaches us about seeing through time. In his book *The Zen of Seeing*, artist Frederick Franck explains that drawing is for him a way to sustain attention, so that a subject can be seen afresh:

> *I have learned that what I have not drawn, I have never really seen, and that when I start drawing an ordinary thing, I realise how extraordinary it is, sheer miracle.*[29]

As a student at Camberwell College of Art, I was taught how to see afresh through the practice of 'blind contour drawing'. Originally defined by the art teacher Kimon Nicolaides in his 1941 book *The Natural Way to Draw*, this approach entails making a continuous mark through close, intense and sustained observation of the contours that define a subject. As students we were encouraged to draw without taking our eyes off the subject to look at the drawing. Holding our attention moment to moment in this way opened up a radical shift in perception. Following the contour of our subject, millimetre by millimetre, we increasingly began to trust in the directness of our seeing. Gone were the glib marks of preconception and in their place we began to make intimate drawings that reflected the immediate presence of the subject. Seeing gradually, we discovered that what lay before us was always more remarkable, more particular, more magical than we could ever have preconceived.

Revelation happens within the seer rather than within the subject seen, for it is the sensitivity of the beholder that is awakened through a sustained acquaintance. The 'sheer miracle' of an ordinary thing, or an ordinary person, becomes evident through our seeing becoming undressed by time. Seeing in this way is intimate, tender and surprising.

*

In a letter to the painter Emile Bernard, Cézanne writes:

*Time and contemplation gradually modify our vision and in the end we achieve understanding.*[30]

Searching for the origin of this word 'contemplation' I discovered that it draws meaning from the root *temp* meaning to 'stretch'. In English, this root gives us the word *temporal* relating to the passage of time (of course in French *temp* means 'time'). So contemplation points us to the essential precondition of seeing deeply – attention stretched out in time.

We only have to think of Cézanne's paintings of everyday objects to be reminded of the power of this extended vision. In repeatedly giving time to the same ordinary objects – an apple, a jug, a vase of flowers – he proves to us that nature does not exist in absolute terms. Given time, it reveals itself as something brand new in the moment. Whole and holy. For the root of 'contemplation' also links us to the word 'temple', which was originally a space stretched out and cleared to make way for sacred practice. So perhaps there is something sacred about sustained attention, something in this practice of contemplation that opens us to revelation.

In psychotherapy contemplation is fostered through a rhythm of weekly visits over time. Seeing through the heart over a matter of months, or sometimes years, opens up a radical shift of perception. In our encounters with one another we begin to see what we didn't see before. Through gradual disclosure an irreplaceable particularity begins to register in ways that would simply not be possible in a single consultation. The person beheld becomes rich in detail and vivid in the presence of their becoming.

\*

Seen at a glance Jake is unremarkable. Wearing the same pair of faded black jeans and a smart-casual jacket every week, he sips from a large plastic cup bought from the cafe below. His gaze is mostly averted, from me, but also from himself. It's hard to stay with him because his voice has become so flat and his body so deserted. His story sits between us like an old map of a land long since lost from sight. When he was seven, Jake's parents sent him to boarding school. His younger sisters remained at home to continue their education at the local school. He was the privileged one. Lucky boy.

Jake remembers very little except the moment his mother told him he could choose one of his toys to take with him. One. That was the moment the lights went out. Desert sands rushed in. After the first two nights of crying in his dormitory, Jake learned a life-saving lesson. *Don't cry.* The boys who cried paid a high price for revealing the bewildered loss which burned their eyes. Any evidence of grief was judged 'wet' and harpooned as soon as it surfaced. It wasn't long before Jake sealed up the senses that made him vulnerable to feeling at all.

Encased in a hard shell, Jake's adult life has been one of achievement. He runs his own property development company and enjoys the comforts of a prosperous life. He has found his way to therapy because his second marriage is heading for the rocks.

There are moments in therapy with Jake when I feel utterly lost. He seems caught in a frozen eddy, which cannot flow on. Week after week we find ourselves going over the same ground, but without feeling or insight. We are skimming the surface. Regular as clockwork Jake turns up. He persists. And that's already something. Somewhere in his human navigational system he knows there must be more to life than this.

Jake's decision to come to therapy is evidence of a seed of hope. A very little seed perhaps, but hope none the less. It is a very precious thing, this seed, and it is vital that it finds fertile soil in which to root and grow. So what encourages this hope to blossom? Diagnosis? Hypothesis? Technique? I have come to believe that at the core, it is the faithful vision of the therapist. The faith she holds that in human nature there is always the possibility of new life. We are shaped by our history, but we are always more than our history. We can be born in the moment. At any moment.

The writers of the New Testament describe faith as:

*The substance of things hoped for and the evidence of things not seen.*[31]

As children we instinctively tune in to the 'evidence of things not seen'. We are awake to the twilight of perception where things and experiences are not yet solid, not yet prescribed. Our organs of perception are still vital, so we see the world afresh, as it is being born. This faithfulness of vision underpins all creative endeavour. It upholds the music teacher who journeys with a student from painful early notes to accomplished playing. It sustains the artist as she makes her first marks on a blank canvas, or the writer on the opening page.

As a psychotherapist, I have found that faith in 'the evidence of things not seen' creates a gravitational field that draws together the tiniest specks of original wholeness from the furthest reaches of a person's universe. These fragments of being are not perceptible at first glance. They surface in response to a quality of vision that has become faithful through long exposure to the *other-wise* nature of the human heart.

Sitting with Jake week after week my thoughts, like sheep, are quick to wander. The emptiness in the room is palpable. It is hard not to feel agitated, distracted, bored. Jake seems bored with himself. It's as though he is looking at the wild and intricate topography of his being from an aeroplane window. Glanced at from a distance all he can see is a lifeless desert of uniformity. Jake's boredom interests me. It signals that he has lost faith that there is anything more to be seen or to be experienced, through staying with himself. The word 'bore' originates in the idea of something that has been hollowed out. I feel drawn to this negative shape, as though it were a footprint of a once living presence. Perhaps, I wonder, Jake's boredom is 'the evidence of things not seen'.

The challenge in these early sessions is to hold fast to the faint imprint of this forgotten self, to bear with the lost shape of the man. This beholding is far from passive. It requires an intention to keep Jake firmly in my sights. The more I look, the more I begin to see. I notice how Jake wrings his hands in a poignant gesture of self-soothing when he approaches a painful memory. I see that when he connects to the original shame of his abandonment, he often closes his eyes, as though by shutting off his own vision he could also become invisible to me. I recognise that when he is taking a risk, he often darts a quick look in my direction. I know that when he is trying to grasp something long lost, his voice begins to crack. I begin to spot slight changes in tone, gesture and pace. Step by step the topography of this lost valley of a man reveals itself. The more I see, the less bored Jake seems to be in his own company.

It takes time, many weeks, for my eyes to adjust to the obscurity of Jake's being. Together we are weaving a container strong enough to hold his loss. Our journey together is tentative. Gradually we are rebuilding the shattered trust. Whilst he is surrendering to the experience of being seen, Jake is taking root inside me. I begin to sense the quickening of new life.

\*

New-born stirrings in the human heart arrive like messengers from somewhere beyond us. Kathleen Raine captures this beautifully in her poem 'Scala Coeli':

*We do not see them come,*
*Their great wings furled, their boundless forms infolded*
*Smaller than a poppy seed or grain of corn*
*To enter the dimensions of our world,*
*In time to unfold what in eternity they are,*
*Each a great sun, but dwindled to a star*
*By the distances they have travelled.*[32]

Life often breaks through the concrete of our defences without fanfare, quietly, like morning dew on the lawns of our lives. 'Smaller than a poppy seed', these disturbances of feeling and thought are 'boundless forms infolded'. Distracted by our preconceptions and blinded by the familiar, we do not see them come.

The favoured greeting of angel messengers who are the bearers of emergent truths is 'behold'. The word is used twice in Luke's account of the Annunciation. First to old Elizabeth's husband Zacharias, then to Mary and again later, heralding the holy birth, to the shepherds on the hillside. This angel word signals that something important is happening. We need to stay alert and keep watching. 'Behold' reminds us that to catch the moment of revelation, we must hold our gaze open, so that the tidings within us become vivid and meaningful. We must greet these messengers and give them 'time to unfold what in eternity they are'.

'Beholding' restores that quality of vision through which we are able to 'hold fast', to 'bear with' what we cannot yet see clearly. We hold when there is nothing more that we can do in the face of what lies before us. The tender resolute gaze of the beholder enfolds us like great wings, entreating and helping us to bear the experience, to stay with it.

At times like these I am reminded of T. S. Eliot's 'Four Quartets', with his powerful testament to faithful vision:

*I said to my soul, be still, and wait without hope*
*For hope would be hope for the wrong thing; wait without love,*
*For love would be love of the wrong thing; there is yet faith*
*But the faith and the love are all in the waiting.*[33]

Jake and I wait. Then one day, towards the end of our session, his voice cracks. 'I saw Robert yesterday.' He pauses, as though gathering together every last scrap of courage. 'His mother died. Suddenly. Overnight.' His speech is laboured and pregnant with meaning. 'Out of the blue. She had a heart attack and... just died.' There is a long moment of silence. I feel everything slow down around us. 'He cried,' Jake says eventually. His knuckles are white from the intensity of holding himself in this moment of disclosure. The air is thick with feeling. Something unspeakable has entered the room. A seven-year-old stands between us, eyes wide with alarm.

Jake's fear of exposing this buried part of himself is so great that he cannot tolerate direct questions. The most I can offer, to encourage a safe opening, is to repeat his own words back to him and to change them into questions through the inflection of my voice. 'His mother died?' I say back to him. My voice is open, tender, simple. I am speaking to the boy. My intonation is full of the angel entreaty. *Stay. Do not flee.*

Jake looks at me. A quick dart, to register what this might mean to me, to cry for a lost mother. I pause, allowing what he has said to take hold. The cells of my body seem to unfurl. There is an opening within me. My own children's faces flash into my mind. The thought of a child suddenly and inexplicably separated from his mother is hard to bear. Suddenly my eyes are hot with tears.

A look of concern flashes across Jake's face. He has seen my vulnerability. We sit in silence together, aware that something small but significant has changed between us. This moment of humanity is worth more than any words. For the first time, Jake considers that crying may not in fact be something 'wet'. Something childish, to be boxed away, along with all his toys. It might after all be safe enough, here, to cry. Present to this moment of nativity, we are both shepherds on a hillside.

In Luke's account of the angel visitations, 'behold' is accompanied by the comforting plea 'fear not':

*And the angel said unto them, Fear not: for, behold,*
*I bring you good tidings of great joy.*[34]

When something buried or unbidden surfaces, the impulse is often to flee. It is tempting to nip it in the bud, or move quickly on. We might distract ourselves or rationalise the nascent truth, so that its vitality and particularity are lost in glib generalisation.

Jake's desolation needs to be held. For as long as it takes. We have to resist the impulse to flee, the pull to look away, the desire to move swiftly on. In choosing to behold we refuse to bottle, belittle or scrutinise. 'The faith and the love are all in the waiting.' So we wait. After a while Jake says, 'I sat with him for ages and… he cried.'

That's when I see him surface. A surge of lamentation wells up in his dustbowl body. His head tips back. The source of his own grief opens, saturating the dry-stone pebbles of his eyes so they shine. All at once his lost valley soul begins to ring with the sound of water. This infinitely simple moment of release unlocks years of life-denying shame, validates the most natural of impulses, to cry for a lost mother.

*

The practice of beholding is especially meaningful in the face of grief. In its raw state, loss can be unspeakable, a primal intimation which is more likely to find expression in a shudder, a choke, an upwelling. Grief reveals itself to be the intimate underbelly of our loving. As Antoine de Saint-Exupéry reflected in one of the most memorable lines from *The Little Prince*: 'It is such a secret place, the land of tears.' This terra incognita must not be analysed, dissected or scrutinised. It is indivisible and incomparable. Holy.

Held with tender and steadfast vision, grief released can, in time, herald a new beginning. Artist Rose-Lynn Fisher captures the transformational power of this elemental secretion in a striking series of duotone photographs of tears shed for a myriad of reasons and magnified through a high-resolution microscope:

> *Tears are the medium of our most primal language in moments as unrelenting as death, as basic as hunger, and as complex as rites of passage. They are evidence of our inner life overflowing its boundaries, spilling over into consciousness. Tears spontaneously release us to the possibility of realignment, reunion, catharsis.*[35]

Un-mourned loss often forms an internal wall in the foundations of our being. Losing sight of the wellspring which lies beneath it, we come to believe that loss *is* the ground of our being. Jake's tears open a door to an original life that lies beneath the layers of loss. In the months that follow we explore the lost valleys of his original nature, which have laid buried beneath his disavowed grief.

Jake begins to remember his dreams. Vivid and particular, each one puts on a show, like a miniature theatre revealing the intricate ecology of his lost realm of experience. Faithfully transcribing them in a small green book, he learns not to judge their strangeness. The more he attends to his dreams, the more they visit him. Whole hosts of angel messengers alight on his pillow. To be honest, I didn't see them coming. It's as though his grief has opened up a secret passageway to a lost dimension in which he is whole, vital and full of insight. Jake and I look into the dreams together, like children gazing into rock pools. Encouraged by their extraordinary precision, he begins to feel deeply 'known' by his dreamer self. In time the faithful presence of this inner messenger opens up the possibility that within him there is a knowing and life-giving presence that will never abandon him.

Reconnecting with this wellspring, Jake is increasingly able to bear with the memory of all that he lost. His dog with her white-tipped tail. His younger sisters who always jumped on his bed. His mother with her busy bustle of care. He remembers the toy he asked for (but could not take). His bike.

In time memories return of the young boy who once explored the quiet freedoms of his lakeland childhood, with all its unrepeatable richness of experience. This awakening is not complete. Significant aspects of his early life remain in cold storage, buried too deep to be retrieved. But Jake no longer turns away from himself. He learns to look and to stay with what he sees. And what he begins to see, he learns to cherish.

Touched by tenderness for the lost boy, Jake buys himself a bike. This simple act is a gesture of faith in a future that can now move on.

*

In his 1948 book *Camera in London*, Bill Brandt asserts that it is part of the photographer's job to see more 'intensely' than most people do. He must look at the world as though for the first time. To look in this way requires courage and faith. It takes courage to let go of what we already know, and faith that new life will be forthcoming if we hold on.

Reflecting on these moments of surfacing between two people what strikes me is their utter simplicity and naturalness in the moment. This directness and spontaneity of perception seems to come from somewhere beyond all preconception. In a rather mysterious way, it is the direct consequence of seeing more *intently*.

Holding faith in the possibility of new beginnings, we *intend* to look beyond the defended self, beyond the wounding. Looking in this way is an act of faith, of wonder and of will.

This quality of seeing is powerfully articulated in the ancient Japanese art of *Sumi-e* painting. *Sumi-e* draws on an earlier Chinese tradition in which the painter was not only an artist by profession, but also a 'seer', a person in search of wisdom. A lifetime of practice was dedicated to expressing the ineffable inner quality of things. Painting with ink on rice paper, one brush stroke only is allowed for each mark. Preparatory marks, revisions and decorations are not permitted. The preparation lies in the looking, in gestating the subject so that it becomes intimately known, before the final gesture of ink onto paper is made. The aim is to capture the vital essence of the subject in the moment. These expressions of pure perception arise naturally through immersive contemplation.

The art of beholding through gestation is beautifully articulated by eleventh-century Chinese poet and painter Su Tung-Po (1037–1101):

> *Before painting a bamboo,*
> *it is necessary for the bamboo to grow in your soul.*
> *Then, with a brush in hand and with eyes focused,*
> *The vision will arise.*
> *Capture it immediately and sketch it,*
> *Because it may quickly disappear*
> *Like a wild rabbit when a hunter is approaching.*[36]

Sitting with Jake for all those months it was necessary for him to grow in my soul. When the decisive moment came, I was able to 'capture it immediately' because my spirit was already full of him, full of his grief and pregnant with the shape of the beautiful carefree boy who once tumbled down the hills of his moorland home.

At the heart of our beholding is the act of looking with intention and with faith. We intend to look beyond the surface. We have faith in the evidence of things not seen. If our seeing is to lead to revelation, we must make friends with time. As the legendary jazz trumpeter Miles Davis once said:

*Man, sometimes it takes you a long time to sound like yourself.*[37]

# CHAPTER THREE

# A MOVING IMAGE

*Sam's story ~ 'The garden of magical possibilities'*

*You don't see the garden as a whole from any point, but you begin to know it by making a tour around it. Then it becomes a garden in the mind, and you become the instrument that defines it.*[38]

Stanley Kunitz

A short walk from my home in South London there is a patch of green surrounded by local shops and a post office. Children play here after school and residents from nearby streets sit awhile and enjoy the shade of an old willow tree. The tree's girth is broad and her foliage generous. She has seen many winters and pours herself out each spring in waterfalls of light.

I have come to know this willow intimately over the years. Approaching her from many different directions, I have seen how her relationship to her surroundings changes with each step, with each shift in perspective. The tree's presence is infused by memories of countless encounters. Sometimes I have sat on the little bench that faces towards her and enjoyed the company of one of my elderly neighbours. In their eyes she seems to offer a steady presence in an unsteady world. When my children were young, I saw her through their eyes. To them she was a playground. Her curtain of green marked a boundary between the visible world of adults and a hidden realm alive with imaginal possibilities. Cradled in my memory and cherished in my imagination, I realise that my vision of the willow is compound. A ragged edged patchwork of moments of seeing.

Turning the corner onto the green one crisp autumn day I feel my heart stop. The tree stands truncated, her majesty reduced to a torso of stumps. She looks neat, in a tortured sort of way. Scalped. Without her branches she can no longer speak. Rigid stupidity replaces the eloquence of her rustling, whispering and weeping. An elderly man stands looking at her, his face wrought with incomprehension. Weeks later, in response to my enquiry, I receive a letter from the council's environment department. It explains that 'the pruning was necessary to avoid excessive leaf litter'.

The council officer's vision of the tree, whilst well meaning, was distant, instrumental and singular. He had not seen the tree through innumerable moments of encounter. He was not moved by the willow's vital distinction, her countless ever-changing dimensions. It struck me then: we harm what we fail to comprehend. The word 'comprehend' combines the Latin *com* ('together') and *prehendere* ('to grasp'). To comprehend something, we allow our multiple impressions of it to be held together simultaneously, without trying to tie it down to any singularity. Its many faces coexist in a collage of coherence.

The intricate wholeness and distinction of a person's life also shows itself in a collage of revelation. In our rush to nail a diagnosis for our suffering, we risk settling for a fixed impression through a singular lens. We become like the council employee who sees only a problem and fails to comprehend the ever-changing complexity, the vital integrity, of a sentient subject. To build a true picture of someone, we hold together a myriad of impressions from different points of view. Together these create the lived distinction of the person in our mind's eye. This shimmering wholeness reveals itself, in the words of Paul Cézanne, as a 'flickering universe, the hesitation of things.'[39]

*

Sam arrives late for our first session. She hauls herself through the door like a seal lumbering onto shore. Landing heavily in the chair, she looks out of the window. She doesn't want to be here, to account for herself all over again. She just wants it all to stop.

Cutting across my opening words, Sam interjects 'I know what's wrong with me. *Mixed Anxiety and Depressive Disorder.*' There is a note of challenge in her voice, a warning perhaps to let me know that this is all wrapped up and I am not to start meddling. 'I found an article about it on the internet. Apparently it affects one in seven people in the UK. It stems from failures in early attachment.'

Sam sees herself through the lens of developmental psychology, a perspective familiar to her from years spent in and out of mental health services. She takes a short breath before completing this well-worn account of her life. 'My mother was an alcoholic. I was in foster care for a time. Until she got clean. We never had much chance to bond properly when I was little.' Her speech is fast, her sentences short and jagged, like forks of lightning. 'Anyway...', she concludes, tying the knot firmly on the story, '... it's all history now.'

Wrapped up in the idea of developmental trauma, Sam feels damaged beyond repair. Sensing that her diagnosis is part of the problem, I suggest that we leave it aside for now. This single-lensed self-perception, with its damning acronym MADD, simply does not do justice to the dynamic particularity of her presence with me. 'That's one way of looking at things,' I say. We could shift perspective a little. Instead of focussing on what may have *gone wrong*, we could explore *who she most essentially is*. Sam looks baffled. She has always just been a problem. It has never occurred to her that she could *be* somebody.

I ask Sam how she experiences her life at the moment. 'People find me annoying,' she says with barely disguised sadness and self-loathing. 'There's always been something weird about me. I'm too sensitive, too intense, too fast. Too everything.' Sam's 'weirdness' has become hard to bear. Burdened with shame, she is haunted by thoughts of self-harm. Asked when the feeling of being weird began, Sam cites her transition to secondary school. 'I just didn't fit in,' she tells me. 'I wasn't interested in all the girl stuff. Most of the time I hid away in the library and read books. In stories you can wander wherever you like and be whoever you want. Nobody minds.' Her smile takes me by surprise. It spreads itself across her face like an upturned rainbow, a fragile wash of colour against dark storm clouds. With mischief in her voice, she adds, 'The possibilities are endless.'

Appealing to this glimpse of glee, I ask Sam if she can remember a favourite story. She pauses, searching my face to see if this might be a trick question. 'There was one. I kept it by my bed for years. Even now I look at it sometimes. You probably know it. *The Secret Garden*. It's the story of a girl, Mary. She finds a walled garden. Long since forgotten and abandoned, it's wild and overgrown. Later she takes her cousin there. He's an invalid. Nobody cares about him. He's been shut away for years. Being in the garden brings him back to life.' In this moment of disclosure we both know that Sam has allowed me to catch a glimpse over her wall. A fledgling thought flits across my inner vision. I wonder if there is a part of Sam that feels invalid. I turn the word over in my mind. *Invalid*. Not only something frail but something illegitimate. In-valid.

Feeling my way forward, I ask Sam if she would be willing to show me around this garden, to take me there, as though we were both in the story. I tell her I'd like to see it through her eyes. Released from the straitjacket of her diagnosis Sam is off and away. Her description of the garden opens onto a never-ending branching of imagery and metaphor. Listening to her, I am struck by the extraordinary fluency and creativity of her mind.

The picture Sam paints is infused with a sense of wonder and abundance. Sensing she is painting a self-portrait, I ask her to take me to the very centre of the garden. 'Beyond the roses, on the other side of the herb garden, there's a fountain,' she tells me. 'It's incredibly beautiful.' Inwardly I smile. At last, we are getting close to the heart of who she really is. Sam's fountain springs forth in a never-ending cascade, each droplet a sparkling orb that holds a whole world in its circumference. 'Sounds magical,' I say. Sam looks straight at me. We both know that the magic has something to do with her.

As we approach the end of the session, I ask Sam if we can make our way back to the garden's secret entrance. I'm curious to see what happens when she returns to the world outside its sheltering walls. All at once, the brightness of her face clouds over. Away from the garden, with its fountain, the magic fades, she tells me. Beyond its walls everything seems barren, flat and lifeless. Looking towards this space she feels a surge of panic, as though she is entering an airless place. 'I don't belong there. Away from the fountain I feel heavy and unable to move. I want to get away as quickly as I can. Back to the fountain.'

Walking around Sam's garden and discovering the fountain at its heart, a new perspective on her suffering begins to open up. I find myself wondering if Sam's fluid intelligence could be the expression of her essential being, a way of experiencing herself that is original, rather than adaptive or damaged. Setting aside the perspective of developmental psychology, with its focus on failures in *nurture*, I suggest we look at her story from a different point of view, through a lens that enquires into her original *nature* as a highly intuitive person.

*

Long before neuroscience revealed two fundamentally contrasted modes of perception, shaped by the left and right hemispheres of the brain, Jung formulated eight personality types based on our innate predispositions. We are perhaps most familiar with these divergent modes through the idea that each of us is oriented towards either extraversion or introversion. Jung also proposed that we are born disposed towards either 'sensation' or 'intuition'. This innate bias can be mild and inconsequential or pronounced and life-defining. Each mode presents both gifts and challenges. Neither is right or wrong. They are just different.

People born with a *sensate* nature rely on evidence from the senses and process perceptual information in an essentially deductive way. They are adept at navigating the literal, the material and the external. By contrast, *intuitive* people draw on imagination to process information through a living web of interrelationships. Their experience is complex, fluid and expansive. Drawn towards nuance, intricacy and the between-ness of things, they are immersed in a world of infinite possibilities:

*Intuition gives outlook and insight; it revels in the garden of magical possibilities as if they were real.*[40]

Sam's fertile imagination opens onto a hinterland of infinite ideas and possibilities. I explain to her that the gifts of an intuitive nature are insight (the ability to look over walls, beyond the defined surface of things) and a fluid intelligence (which connects discreet facts into a web of dynamic relationships). Her face lights up. Secretly she knows this already.

Sam's intuitive nature also presents her with specific challenges. Her insight, with its abundance and fluidity, can be dazzling, seductive and intoxicating. In the shadow of her magical interior, the world of concrete facts, singular pathways and prescribed rules of behaviour feel exhausting and frustrating. Away from her imagination, Sam tells me, she feels reduced, deadened and anxious. A fish out of water. Hearing this image of herself, I begin to understand the pain behind the disengaged creature who first lumbered onto my shore.

The challenges of relating to the world at large are often masked in childhood precisely because the inner world of imagination is valued in our early years. As the child enters secondary school, she encounters the challenge of forming mature relationships. The naturally wandering and wondering intuitive mind struggles to gain purchase on the increasingly narrow train tracks of socially acceptable behaviour. Confronted by a society increasingly defined by self-evident facts and rational logic, it can be tempting for the intuitive person to retreat into their more vital and fluid inner experience. She may begin to feel out of step. Different. Weird.

*

By exploring who Sam most essentially is, we begin to form a picture of her life that looks through the lenses of *nature* as well as *nurture*. Her distress may indeed originate in 'failures in early attachment', but it may also be an expression of challenges arising from her intuitive nature. Her depression expresses the loss of infinite possibility which she experiences whenever she has to function in the finite and imperfect material world. Her anxiety may be the consequence of childhood experiences of neglect, but it may *also* be the consequence of the exponential branching system of her right brain processing. In the fast-flowing currents of her mind, a negative thought can mushroom into a thousand off-shoots in a matter of moments. Unchecked, a painful memory can multiply exponentially. The fountain can quickly become a flood.

Seen through the lens of developmental psychology, the anxiety that arises from engagement with the world can easily be regarded as a dysfunction, a disorder. Through the singular certainty of this perspective, with its hard and fast diagnostic labelling, Sam's fluid and intricate intelligence has become a disability born of 'failures in her maternal care environment'. Her way of being registers as invalid, a source of shame.

Exploring her life story from different perspectives, Sam discovers that she is not just a problem to be fixed. She is alive, complex and gifted. Her identification with the magical fountain gives us a clear view of her extraordinary fluid intelligence. It also offers us fresh insight into the underlying sense of alienation she has felt since childhood. As a highly sensitive, introverted and intuitive person she has indeed been out of step in a world which champions extroversion and rational evidence-based perception. Her need to retreat into the freedom of her imagination has been too easily pathologized.

Seeing herself from the perspective of her original nature, the toxic shame which has polluted Sam's wellbeing for so many years begins to clear. Thoughts of self-harm are replaced by a wish to cherish and cultivate the gifts of her innate way of being. Her nature becomes different, magical even. And certainly not just 'weird'.

In the months ahead we begin to explore how Sam can move safely between this magical inner space and the outer world which feels so alien to her. Building on her sense of herself as a fish out of water, I suggest she might be like a diver who needs to rise slowly from the deep ocean, to avoid the 'bends'. Sam's nature orientates her towards depth and absorption, so she often loses track of time and space. She needs a thread, an umbilical cord, which will tug when it's time to return to the surface.

Sam begins to write. She writes every day, for just half an hour. At first she struggles with the limitation imposed by this structure. With gentle curiosity we explore how it feels to interrupt her flow, to return to the surface. Sam discovers that she needs time to transition from one state to another. She learns to take responsibility for her gift, to tend and care for intuitive nature.

\*

Our seeing is shaped as much by our perspectives, belief systems and ideas as it is by the evidence of our senses. Jungian psychologist James Hillman refers to ideas as the 'eyes of the soul':

> *Without them we cannot 'see' even what we sense with the eyes in our heads, for our perceptions are shaped according to particular ideas. Once we considered the world flat and now we consider it round; once we observed the sun rotate around the earth, and now we observe the earth turn round the sun; our eyes, and their perceptions did not change with the Renaissance. But our ideas have changed and with them what we 'see'.[41]*

The word *idea* itself comes from the Greek word for seeing, *eidos*, which originally meant both that which one sees (a vision) and the lens through which we see (the faculty of vision). Understood in this light, ideas are windows through which our seeing is shaped. The more vibrant and various our ideas, the more alive and complete our seeing will be. Where ideas become concrete and stale, they mask our vision, blinding us to dimensions which are perhaps more complex, subtle or hidden. The myriad shadings of human experience remain undiscovered, uninitiated and unloved.

Contemporary psychology is awash with different conceptual lenses, so we might assume that our seeing of human experience would be rich, textured and intricate. Instead, specialisation within mental health risks leading us towards a splintering of perception. We are increasingly seduced by one-eyed monsters proffering psychological approaches which lay claim to a completeness of vision from a singular point of view: psychodynamic, cognitive behavioural, somatic trauma-focussed, mentalisation-based, Jungian – the list goes on. Each of these perspectives has value, but as exclusive aspects none come close to a wholeness of vision.

Reflecting on the plethora of singular perspectives which dominate the field of contemporary psychology, it occurs to me that we have perhaps arrived at the same impasse that confronted artists in the early twentieth century. Frustrated by the limitations of a kind of 'tripod vision', artists like Picasso and Braque developed a new compound vision which challenged the singular perspective and its seamless view.

In June 1930 Picasso purchased an eighteenth-century château in Normandy. 'Boisgeloup' provided a welcome retreat from public life. It also served as place for secret meetings with his lover Marie-Thérèse Walter. In the months that followed he turned one of the stables into a sculpture studio. Here he began to develop a radical new visual language. Attending to his subject from multiple points of view, he transformed Marie-Thérèse's features into three-dimensional volumes. Beyond sculpture, this new compound vision was to surface in an outpouring of astounding paintings. In 1932 Picasso produced a series of pictures of reclining nudes in which he simultaneously incorporated multiple perspectives of his subject. In a radical shift he broke free from the seamless view that had dominated Western perception for three hundred years.

The full power of this compound way of seeing is evident in Picasso's 1937 depiction of the bombing of the Basque town Guernica by German forces in the Spanish Civil War. In this monumental composition Picasso returned to the broad format of the mural to bring together (to 'comprehend') a jarring dissonance of different perspectives and emotional responses. It's possible that Picasso conceived this work by pulling together the many shocking pictures of devastation that appeared as black and white photographs in newspapers. Holding together a myriad of dissonant images, he produced a composite vision of hell.

At first glance the painting appears confusing and chaotic. The space fractures around the multiple viewpoints characteristic of Picasso's cubist style. Images overlap and intersect, their forms discontinuous and fragmented. Standing in front of this monumental work our seeing moves from figure to figure, looking out on the scene through multiple pairs of anguished eyes. We cannot remain fixed in any single viewpoint. We have to enter in. The viewer is immersed in a visceral reality of the destructive chaos of war. In this extraordinary painting we sense the sustained attention of a beholder who walks around the horror and is profoundly *moved*.

In challenging the authority of the exclusive aspect, Picasso drew on experiments by artists of the time with collage (from French *coller,* meaning to stick together). This composite approach helped dispel the idea that a true representation requires a single seamless plane of vision. Collage involves combining disparate elements and accepting the discontinuous texture that results. The joins and discontinuities between different perspectives no longer matter in the representation of the whole. Rather the overlaps and ragged edges, the dissonance and clashes define the realness of the living subject.

These experiments with compound vision drew inspiration from other cultures where perception has always stemmed from a moving encounter. In China the scroll dominated perception and depiction for centuries. Stretched beyond the limits of a narrow frame, Chinese scrolls and screens invite the viewer to enter into the image, as though retracing the steps and ever-changing viewpoints of the artist. This extension of vision requires the viewer to take in the subject from many different standpoints.

In other parts of Asia temple murals extended over hundreds of metres, depicting moving scenes of extraordinary perceptual complexity. Perhaps the most famous of these is the breathtaking gallery of bas-reliefs surrounding the first level of the Angkor Wat temple, built in the twelfth century deep in the Cambodian jungle. Here 1,200 square metres of sandstone carvings move in one unbroken visual narrative of myth and history. These temple carvings are alive with movement and drama because they incorporate a different point of view at every point of depiction. Without the fixed lens of a camera, there is no singular vanishing point. We find ourselves looking from multiple perspectives simultaneously.

Contemporary British artist David Hockney reimagined this art of compound vision when, between 1981 and 1983, he created hundreds of photographic collages. Hockney made these *Joiners* in reaction to the fixed view of what he called 'the paralysed Cyclops', a singular perspective which he attributed to the proliferation of photography. These collage experiments produce pictures charged with a vital energy and authenticity. We the viewer move around the subject. We become part of the dynamic, which is at the heart of perception. The shimmering relationship of beholder and beheld.

\*

Anyone who has ever sat and watched dragonflies flying over a pond, turning back and forth in an iridescent display of aerial acrobatics, will not be surprised to learn that they have wrap-around vision. They can see in virtually all directions at the same time. Their large compound eyes are composed of many tiny little facets called *ommatidia*. Amazingly there are up to 30,000 of these lenses, each giving a fractionally different perspective. This prism creates a collage of partially overlapping images, which are held together within the brain. Within human experience, we are perhaps most familiar with this dragonfly vision in the complex dramas presented to us by our imagination in dreams.

From the perspective of our rational minds these shape-shifting visions don't seem to 'add up'. We are quick to dismiss them as nonsense, or else we pick out some features, whilst discounting the more bizarre anomalies. On waking it usually feels as though there is a subject dreamer who experiences from a singular perspective. Re-entering a dream with compound vision, we discover a drama infinitely more faceted in which our imagination takes multiple positions simultaneously.

This dragonfly vision is powerfully illustrated in a dream Sam shares with me several months after our first encounter:

*I am standing on the seashore looking out at a huge ocean. Something about the sea unsettles me. At the far end of the beach I can just see a woman in a pink bikini standing amongst a group of friends. She is animated and laughing loudly as she entertains the others with a tale of some kind. They are all spellbound. Out of the corner of my eye I suddenly notice in the sea a small child in a rubber ring. Somehow I know this is the woman's child. She is quiet, passive. The water is withdrawing, pulling the child further and further out to sea. I run towards the woman, screaming. But she cannot hear me. Then the ocean heaves in one gigantic motion and the child is pulled up by an enormous wave. I wake with a feeling of absolute terror.*

I suggest to Sam that all the dream's characters are different perspectives (like the dragonfly's ommatidia) on her own complex story. We agree to walk around these different points of view together.

First, Sam explores the perspective of the dreamer. She describes her unsettling premonition, with its sudden apprehension of danger, her powerlessness to reach the mother or the child. From this position, the sea appears dangerous and ruthless and she feels impotent. Shifting perspectives, I invite Sam to take the position of the woman on the beach. I ask about the *pink* bikini, a marginal but curiously specific detail. She tells me that as a child she was always dressed in pink by her mother. Perhaps, she reflects, the woman in pink represents a way of being that originated in childhood. Standing in her shoes, Sam connects to a deep and shameful truth. 'To distract myself from scary things I used to tell myself stories. I would take myself on an adventure in my mind to block out whatever was happening around me.'

Next we move to take the perspective of the child at sea, the girl untethered from her mother's attention, enclosed by her rubber ring, yet apparently in mortal danger. Seeing through the eyes of the child, Sam recognises a deep numbness. It's as though her instincts are switched off. Noticing this disconnection, a buried memory begins to resurface. When Sam's mother was in the grip of her alcohol dependency, a new man entered their lives. 'I was eight or nine at the time. It was the year before I went into foster care.' Her mother's boyfriend became part of her circle of care, her rubber ring. 'He used to buy me sweets. He made me feel special. I remember thinking I should be grateful.' So when he visited Sam's room late at night, whilst her wine-soaked mother sat downstairs, Sam would tell herself a little story to numb out the swell of fear within. Her instinctual self knew something was wrong, very wrong, but she could not risk letting this truth in. If she made a fuss, things could get a lot worse.

The following week I ask Sam if she would be willing to re-enter the dream and take the perspective of the sea itself. 'The sea?' she questions. It hasn't occurred to Sam that the sea could hold a position in the dream. Breathing deeply, she closes her eyes. Her whole body seems to expand, as though suddenly filling up. She looks agitated and her voice becomes strong and urgent. 'I am swelling around the child, but I am also somehow inside the child. I am trying to warn her, but the child can't hear me. She's in real danger! Why won't she cry out to her mother?'

Identifying as the sea, Sam begins to tune in to its intelligence, to feel the urgency of its alarm. This new perspective opens up a blind spot in Sam's story. The wave, it seems, is the instinctual cry the child was unable to make. It lifts the child up, not to carry her away, but rather to draw attention to her vulnerability. There is a parallel between the woman in pink not hearing the dreamer's calls of alarm and the child not hearing the voice of the sea. Through fear the child distracted herself from the swell of emotional disturbance within. She turned off the very alarm system that could have protected her. No wonder the world of relating has felt so bewildering and so dangerous. No wonder she has found sanctuary in an imaginal realm, which has felt safe and beautiful and kind.

Through the many different perspectives of her dream, Sam begins to recognise the intelligence of her inner ocean. She recovers an essential navigational tool, an instinctual alarm system that has been switched off since childhood. The dream's lifesaving message only becomes visible when seen from multiple points of view.

During the course of our work together, Sam sees herself through a host of different perspectives. We are careful not to discard the original insight into her suffering, rooted as it is in very real failures in her early attachments. We have to bear the possibility that we may never be able to join these different perspectives into a single seamless view.

*

Like Sam, each of us can only be comprehended as a sum of multiple perspectives. At the same time we are always more than this sum. When this collaged wholeness registers in our sight, we encounter a holiness of perception. Both 'whole' and 'holy' share the same old English root in the word *halig*, which carries the idea of something that is essentially intact, inviolate. We violate the integrity of human experience when we paint over inconsistencies and discard the pieces that don't fit our theoretical model, when we privilege one aspect over another.

What Picasso, Hockney and the acrobatic dragonfly have taught me is that we can hold multiple perspectives simultaneously. Through compound vision, with its collage of perspectives, we confront the challenge of perceiving the complexity of human experience, without needing to collapse it into a monocular theory or rigid diagnosis. We may have to bear the tension between viewpoints that don't neatly add up. These untidy joins keep our seeing honest, alive and meaningful.

To behold the flickering universe of human nature, we need a moving enquiry, one in which we acknowledge the fundamental incompleteness of our field of view. The hidden wonders of the human heart cannot be seen by looking through the window of singular certainty. They will not yield to this exclusive viewpoint. The wholeness of human nature lies at the edges of knowing. In the spaces between the familiar forms. In the negative shapes of our being.

# CHAPTER FOUR

# THE HIDDEN FACE

*Ralph's story ~ 'Totems of toughness'*

*Everyone is a moon, and has a dark side*
*which he never shows to anybody.*[42]

Mark Twain

Ralph tells me he has come to therapy to learn how to be more resilient. His broad frame perches awkwardly, as though the softness of the chair threatens to emasculate him. Arms heavy with a calligraphy of tattoos – serpents, skulls, a bird of prey – every inch of his body communicates toughness. Only his eyes give him away. His look is haunted, as though a ghost stalks through the inner chambers of his being. I have a creature in the room. One false move from me and he will be off.

The record company Ralph works for operates in a competitive market. Its staff are rewarded for high-octane performance and long hours. Like his colleagues, Ralph works hard and plays hard. In recent months his sleep has been disturbed by night terrors, which can no longer be assuaged through drinking. He feels he has reached a breaking point.

Ralph blames himself *for not being tougher.* This brings us to the heart of the matter. For Ralph is always trying to be tougher. The only alternative he sees to being tough is to give in to being weak. 'What might it look like, to be more resilient?' I ask. Perplexed by the question, Ralph replies, 'I'd be able take the heat, like everyone else.' I feel him bristle with irritation. He wants solutions from me, not daft questions. 'How do you take the heat at the moment?' I persist. Looking me straight in the eye he replies, 'I just keep going. I try harder.'

Ralph is like a moon unable to turn away from the sun. It simply hasn't occurred to him that there might be a natural limit to the amount of heat he can take. All around him business goes on as usual. Competition in the marketplace keeps getting hotter. Everyone is stressed. They just have to deal with it. Resilience in this relentlessly ratcheted environment begins to fail. Under the skin, beneath the protective totems of toughness, Ralph is beginning to crack. His intimate anguish unfolds out of sight. The face he presents to the world is indestructible.

Ralph's tattoos intrigue me. What might these sentinels be guarding, I wonder. What treasure might warrant this level of protection? I sense that his encrypted skin marks a shared contour between the face he presents to the world and a hidden face. What life of great and tender worth might lie on the other side of this mighty shield?

T. S. Eliot calls this concealed dimension 'a face still forming'. He reminds us that this face is not inherently obscure. It is 'Not known, because not looked for.'[43]

*

As a child looking at the moon wax and wane, I imagined an enormous biscuit being slowly devoured by a hungry and invisible being. Where her fullness once shone, an indistinct blackness bleached into the background expanse of the dark universe. Now I understand that the moon is always whole. We just don't see all of her because we are drawn to her illuminated aspect. Knowing this now, I take delight in training my eyes to look for the negative shape of her wholeness. Sometimes, tenderly cupped in her crescent, I catch a glimpse of an inverse moon. I begin to see that her two faces are intimately related in an ever-changing dance of reciprocity. The hidden face is not indistinct, but rather follows a particular contour, which is the exact inverse of her sunlit shape.

Dutch artist M. C. Escher famously represented this complementary interface of perception in pictures which challenge us to look equally at 'positive' and 'negative' shapes. In his 1938 woodcut 'Sky and Water', for example, our attention is drawn at the bottom of the picture to the lighter forms of fish set against a dark background. As our eyes move up the work, Escher gradually articulates this dark 'background', so that it takes a recognisable form. Gradually we become aware of the negative space between the fish. At the top of the picture, these negative shapes can be seen as a flock of birds.

The longer we look at an Escher print the more we begin to realise that the contour of the inverse shape has an intricate precision in the way that it relates to the more identifiable form. His images remind us that by focusing on the interface where these inverse realities meet, we can begin to appreciate that everything in fact fits together in pairs of reciprocities. The unarticulated space is merely the inverse of the recognisable form. Negative and positive spaces create each other.

Before the cementing of adult perception in the concrete visual language of recognition (re-cognition), children draw pictures in which both foreground and background are equally observed. Because the whole subject before them is yet to be known, the form and the formless space remain equally important. So, when drawing a tree, they will faithfully draw the shape of the sky between the branches. Adult beginners in drawing often lavish attention on the recognisable forms and rush to fill in the 'background'. Areas of the whole that are not named are largely ignored or approximated rather than observed. These drawings are invariably less acutely perceived, less vital and less true to the distinction of the subject.

In her book *Drawing on the Right Side of the Brain*, Betty Edwards reminds us that negative space is simply the aspect that the eye does not focus on. She demonstrates that by drawing the shapes we *do not recognise,* we arrive at an immeasurably more accurate representation of the subject as a whole.

As a photographer I have always found the negative image incredibly beautiful. In a photographic negative all the brightest light sources appear as the darkest areas and the darkest areas as the lightest. The resulting inverse image presents the same subject in ways that highlight the space between recognised shapes, the space we typically dismiss as background.

To develop a negative into a recognisable print I first *reverse* it so that the background becomes the subject. Then I *enlarge* the negative and *focus* it onto light-sensitive paper. Finally, I place it in *developing* solution for just the right amount of time, so that it is neither over nor under exposed. Rather beautifully, this is also what I do as a therapist with the 'negative' image of my clients' stories. Together we enlarge the disregarded dimension by giving it space in our attention. The more we look at it, the brighter its distinct value and form register, the more we begin to see how exactly it completes the known story.

\*

The landscape of human experience is lunar. Our sense of self is shaped through stories that are well lit, having turned many times in the orbit of our attention. We are pattern-making creatures after all. Our seeing is drawn to recognition. We are easily frustrated, stressed even, by aspects that are indeterminate or in a state of flux. Eclipsed by the solid shape of the known, the unfamiliar reaches of being register dimly as an indistinct background.

British psychoanalyst Christopher Bollas refers to this hidden face as the 'unthought known',[44] a prescient hinterland of inarticulate feelings, forbidden thoughts, disavowed longings and emergent possibilities. These are known to us at some level, but have either been buried away from awareness, or have yet to be brought to mind. They remain 'undrawn'.

Artists, writers and poets across the ages have understood that this dimly lit realm of human experience is not just an indistinct blank, nor merely a primitive unconscious. In its furthest reaches, this 'unthought known' is shot through with intelligible lucidity. French poet and novelist Victor Hugo refers to it as a realm of '*dark radiance*':

> ... *the luminous world is the invisible world;*
> *the luminous world is that which we do not see.*
> *Our eyes of flesh see only night.*[45]

'That which we do not see' is not blank or approximate, but luminous, particular and pregnant with implicate knowing. A seedbed of possibility, it carries our deepest recollections of an original state of wholeness. At the same time, it holds the blueprint of who we are meant to be. To see into this dark radiance we must train our vision to draw out the particular shape and quality of background space. We look for the inverse self.

This reversal of vision is harder than it might appear. Increasingly we seem fixated on a small number of illuminated aspects. *Happiness, success* and *strength* have become the benchmarks of human worth and wellbeing. Focused only on these 'positive' emotional monoliths, all we see beyond is an indistinct background, a formless void. Instead of looking directly and particularly at the other side of 'happy' or 'successful', we tend to negate it by adding the prefix 'un'. This gives us bland binary configurations like happy and *un-happy*, successful and *un-successful*, which tells us nothing about the particular shape of the 'negative' state. Seen in this way we disregard anything which isn't happy as failure, as illegitimate and unhealthy. Like Ralph we believe that if we are not *strong* then we must be *weak*. Our 'negative shape', the dark side of our moon, registers as invalid. A source of shame. No wonder we look away.

But the inverse of *happy* cannot be discerned simply by negating it. The absence of *happy* is not just a blank space. It has a finely delineated shape, which expresses a particular pattern of emotional intelligence. This undrawn shape might be *disappointed, frustrated, bereft, bewildered, melancholy*, or *yearning*, to name but a few possibilities. Similarly, the complementary inverse of *strong* is not simply *weak*. It could be *tender, delicate, sensitive, intricate, slight, gentle, fragile, or vulnerable*. Each of these states has its own value, its own particular purpose and quality. Our vulnerability opens us to the richness of human experience, to the subtle wisdom of our deep intelligence. Our tenderness awakens our compassion for each other. Our yearning makes vivid what we value. Melancholy was understood in the Renaissance as a window to the soul, a state of deep reflection necessary to pass through certain states of spiritual evolution.

*

At other times and in different cultures, seeing into the human condition has explicitly included the idea of the inverse face, the completing shape. For the Igbo people of south-eastern Nigeria, each distinct quality of human experience is inextricably related to a reciprocal quality which must be discerned, welcomed and cultivated, to make the person whole.

In the novels of Chinua Achebe and Chigozie Obioma we learn that within Igbo culture the idea of singular absolute aspects is unthinkable. Alongside any quality or value, there always stands a complementary 'otherness'. This principle is encapsulated in the

Igbo proverb *'Ife kwulu, ife akwudebe ya'*, meaning 'where one thing stands, something else stands beside it'. Understood in this way nothing has value to the exclusion of its inverse quality. So the masculine is defined by its relationship to the feminine, light to dark, joy to sadness, strength to vulnerability. These pairings are not oppositional or hierarchical; they are balancing and completing.

Where everything coexists within pairings of beneficial reciprocity, it follows that:

> ... any aspect which is ignored, denigrated, denied acknowledgement and celebration can become the focus of anxiety and disruption.[46]

The harm caused through seeing only one side of a pairing is played out in Chinua Achebe's celebrated novel *Things Fall Apart*. Published in 1958, its story chronicles pre-colonial life in south-eastern Nigeria and the arrival of the Europeans during the late nineteenth century. In this tale, the Igbo protagonist Okonkwo breaks with the holistic vision that is the cornerstone of his culture. Ashamed of his father's penury he blames this unfortunate state on the man's lack of strength, a quality he interprets as *weakness*. Fearful of this perceived weakness Okonkwo strives at all times to exhibit heroic courage and demonstrate physical strength and dominance. Without the 'something else' of his dual nature, Okonkwo is quite lost. His exclusive focus on strength robs him of the values of gentleness and sensitivity, which might have allowed him to respond to the European threat with a more subtle and reflective wisdom. In the end his family falls apart. It crumbles, Achebe suggests, not because of conflict with colonial values, but rather from an imbalance within.

In my therapy practice I am on the lookout for the 'something else' that lies on the other side of the illuminated known. This negative shape may seem to lie beyond the reach of ordinary perception, until we remember that it shares an interface with the aspect we can see. If a person demonstrates a strong pattern of compliance, I might begin to wonder about their hidden disobedience. Someone puffed up with self-importance may be concealing aspects of their being which feel small or insignificant.

Sitting with Ralph, my starting point is to attend to the contours of his illuminated aspect. The strong-man persona. We begin by articulating and exploring the qualities of his tattoo shield – *tough, hard, impenetrable, deflecting, protecting*. Then, looking for the concealed aspect, I suggest that we reverse the tattoo qualities (like a negative in the darkroom). We begin to discern the inverse faces of his toughness – *soft, tender, yielding, revealing, allowing*. Towards the end of this session I suggest to Ralph that he consider if there might be something he secretly wishes to *reveal*, something he longs to *allow*, something he might want to *feel*. Faced with this invitation, I notice Ralph seems agitated. He looks away, as though this night vision might somehow penetrate his shield.

Ralph does not show up for his next session. Nor the one after that. I fear I have lost him. Perhaps I have moved too fast. Perhaps the very possibility of softness frightened him away. The following week, to my surprise, he returns, carrying a battered old shoe box covered in faded stickers. Opening the lid Ralph shows me a roughly packaged pile of cassette tapes, a secret hoard of songs, written and recorded when he was fifteen. This is the first time he has opened the box in twenty years. There it is. His hidden treasure.

Over the following weeks, Ralph begins to disclose the forsaken aspect of his life. When he was fourteen he woke up one morning to find his father missing from the breakfast table. A neatly written note explained that he had left the family home to pursue a relationship with a woman he had met the year before at a conference in Germany.

Ralph's mother told him his father was 'a lousy piece of shit' and they were better off without him. He would soon get over it. In the long days that followed, she soldiered on, defiantly modelling a kind of stoic fortitude. Bewildered and bereft, Ralph found himself stepping into his father's shoes, being the man around the house, looking out for his mother and three sisters. For all their sakes, he had to be strong.

In the concealed safety of his bedroom the tender adolescent survived – for a while. Wrapped around his guitar he wrote songs about anger and fear, about loss and about love. Music stopped him dying inside. No one listened. Hollowed out with forbidden grief for his abandoning father, Ralph's emotional world, like his songs, remained hidden in a box. Shameful evidence of his 'weakness'. Increasingly he found himself in trouble at school. He got into fights and began taking drugs. They helped to block out his vulnerability, his forbidden feelings. Despite his obvious intelligence he left at sixteen with only a handful of exam passes. In the years since then he has buried his tender self within the music industry, walking through life as a shadow artist, toughing it out organising gigs and record deals for musicians with half his raw talent.

Some weeks later Ralph asks if I would like to hear one of his songs. He has brought with him an old cassette player. Slowly, with great care, he presses the red button to 'play'. A rough and tender voice pierces the space between us. It is shot through with the raw edge of adolescent loss and yearning. The song is both sensitive and strong. It moves me. Ralph observes me intently. He sees that I'm affected by his music. He knows then that something about his expression of feeling is good. Listening to these songs together, Ralph and I begin to sense that *tenderness* (not *weakness*) is the 'something else', the undrawn face, which lies on the other side of his armoured strength.

Over time, through reconnecting to his music, Ralph dares to face the concealed truth. He loves his father. He misses him every day. He is surprised to discover that love is a power. It stirs in him with a force that feels unshakeable. This love feels neither feeble nor weak. It is mighty and resolute. He begins to realise that his night terrors contain an imperative, a call to action.

It takes over a year to track his father down.

Six months later, Ralph emails me an audio file. Tender and powerful, it is a new song. He calls it 'Prodigal Blues'.

*

Like so many of us, Ralph turned to therapy to learn how to be more resilient. The word *resilience* originally drew its inspiration from the ebb and flow of natural cycles. In nature resilience operates within organic rhythms of impact and restoration. In this context survival depends on a combination of *sensitivity and strength*. Sensitivity alerts the organism to opportunity and to threat, whilst strength allows for some protection and forbearance.

Resilience is built into the natural world, but it is not infinite. Reef-building corals for example, which support an abundance of life in our marine ecologies, live for millennia in a continual cycle of impact and renewal. The living polyps are only a few years old, but they rely on an underlying skeleton that can live for up to four thousand years. These corals can survive short periods of elevated seawater temperatures. Their capacity to manufacture food through photosynthesis is temporarily compromised and they lose their colour. Once the waters cool, they sense the restoration of safe limits and resume the normal processes which return them to their full glory.

In 2016 scientists chronicled a mass mortality on the Australian Great Barrier Reef. Over thirty per cent of the reef's corals died in a catastrophic nine-month marine heatwave. This unspeakable tragedy points to a condition of nature, concerning which we are increasingly in denial. Nature, including human nature, operates *within limits*. Like coral reefs, we too are deformed under excessive stress. The damage begins at the more vulnerable margins, with those of us who are by nature, or through poverty, or by age or youth, more sensitive. But in the end the overheated environmental stresses will affect us all.

Like the oceans, our human ecology is becoming overheated. I am more than ever convinced that the explosion in mental health problems in people of all ages is not a straightforward failure of individual resilience, but a sign that environmental stresses are overwhelming the inherent limits of our nature.

In contemporary society toughness seems to have become the exclusive aspect to which we aspire. We admire 'nerves of steel', 'rock-hard determination' and 'iron ladies.' We 'hammer out' and 'battle through' our problems. We spin the promise that through therapy, mindfulness and other personal growth practices we can withstand the intolerable ratcheting up of societal stresses. This confounding of resilience with a limitless capacity to absorb pressure masks the structural problems behind so much of our suffering.

At this point it seems we have two choices. We calcify, numbing the sentient organs of perception that suffer the stress from over-reaching our limits. Or we begin to crack, to bleach, to fade. The people I worry most about are those who chose to calcify. They are often the ones who head up our corporate organisations and lead our nations. Shorn of their capacity to feel they become a danger to themselves and to others. Increasingly they lead us into war and to the irreparable despoiling of our planet.

Of course, there is a third choice. We could hold the reciprocal qualities of strength and sensitivity in equal regard. We could understand that resilience depends on their intimate correlation.

\*

In the Japanese art of *Kintsukuroi*, broken pottery is repaired with lacquer dusted with gold or silver to emphasise the breaks, to celebrate the reciprocal value of the vessel's vulnerability and of its enduring strength. The beauty of the Kintsukuroi bowl rests in the indisputable truth that in its broken and mended state it is unique. No two pots can be broken in exactly the same way. In these bowls, these incomparable objects, we find an expression of the 'broken wholeness' of our experience. We are reminded that human nature is beautiful, not despite its tender limitations, but because of them. In our broken wholeness, each of us is irreplaceable.

As a community of beings we are in effect all aspects of one indivisible skin, which needs to be both strong enough to protect and sensitive enough to feel. In her book *The Highly Sensitive Person*,[47] Elaine Aron suggests that heightened sensitivity manifests in a certain proportion of all higher species, because it is essential for the survival of the whole group. Sensitivity allows us to pick up subtle and nuanced signs which might herald danger, but which may also fundamentally enrich existence.

Increasingly I see the people who courageously step into the therapy room as equivalents to canaries in the coalmine. Their sensitivity alerts the wider community to rises in the level of psychological toxins and temperatures in our collective environment, which threaten to overwhelm the balance and limits of resilience in our human ecology. If we could begin to listen to these more tender voices, rather than medicating them into dumb silence, if we could stop urging them to toughen up, we might recover qualities of sensitivity that are an essential aspect of our native resilience.

To discern the hidden face, we look beyond the illuminated story. There, in the shadows of human nature we find so much more than broken pieces. We encounter the 'dark radiance' of which Victor Hugo spoke. To see into this uncharted firmament, we need to cultivate a sensitivity of vision that is more than meets the eye.

# CHAPTER FIVE

# A TENDER VISION

*Anita's story ~ 'The nub of coldness'*

*The voices of angels reach us*
*Even now, and we touch one another*
*Sometimes, in love, with hands that are not hands,*
*With immaterial substance, with a body*
*Of interfusing thought, a living eye.*[48]

Kathleen Raine

From her place on the bench Martha watches, transfixed by the elemental power of the lion's great padding paws. He takes four steps forward. Then, with infinite grace, he turns and takes four steps back to the other side of the cage. Over and again he traces this narrow path, back and forth. He cannot, must not, stop moving. To stop would be to open up a space for the full tide of his desolation to pour into the chambers of his big-cat heart. Through the invisible pathway of 'interfusing thought' a young woman is touched by the lived experience of a lion. His slow deliberate movements seem to her a kind of valiant refusal to succumb to the reality of his incarceration. A wave of lamentation rolls through her.

Martha Graham spent many hours at New York City's Central Park Zoo. She was to become one of the great American artists of the twentieth century. An electrifying dancer and influential choreographer, she expressed through movement the joys, passions and sorrows common to all human experience. Bertram Ross, one of her principal dancers, reflected 'Here was somebody who could manifest, make visible, all those feelings that you have inside you that you can't put into words.'[49]

Freeing herself from the orchestrated forms of classical ballet, Martha Graham sought to express the inner world of emotions. She noticed that deep-seated emotional states manifest first in the torso, in the very guts of being. She named this sixth sense 'the house of pelvic truth':

> *Every emotion... starts or is visible in the torso first. The heart pounds, the lungs fill; and if the lungs fill there is a sharp spasm of activity in the ribs and diaphragm, since all life hangs on breath.*[50]

Language reminds us that emotions are embodied movements of the essential currents of life. We might feel *choked* with grief or *bursting* with pride. We *radiate* happiness or we *seethe* with rage. Choked, bursting, radiating and seething are all verbs that speak of a disturbance of energy, which registers first in our bodily senses. Long before we articulate a thought or an emotion, we might feel our guts clench, or our hearts pound. Our skin might pucker-up in goose bumps; our cheeks suddenly flush. Our throats may tighten, our flesh creep or our eyes well up. These are all felt responses to the inchoate ebb and flow of life flowing within and between us. The truth of this gut feeling can be hard to stomach.

Many of Martha Graham's most memorable performances demonstrated how the simplest of movements – a gasp, a sigh, a sob – can communicate an enormous intensity and complexity of feeling. In one of her signature works, 'Lamentation', the harrowing reality of grief is conveyed by a seated figure whose slow and seamless movements rock back and forth with a wordless grace. Perhaps Martha was recalling that moment with the lion when she, seated on the bench, felt a wave of desolation roll through her. Seeing this dance always moves me, because two people in therapy, though seated, communicate great depths of feeling through the 'immaterial' pathways of 'interfusing thought'.

*

Like a bird condemned to ceaseless migration, Anita scans distant horizons for a place to land. Her eyes seem restless and unfocused. All the while, the branch I offer remains undiscovered. The suitcase which accompanies her into therapy today reminds me that she has come to her session straight from the airport. Anita started her day in Milan where she was a keynote speaker at an international conference. Still, she is well prepared for our session. Barely drawing breath, she launches into an account of her week. It's been another busy one.

In therapy, as in life, Anita works hard. She has turned to therapy to figure out why she can't find a lasting relationship. Week after week she arrives longing for revelation. Her notebook bulges with self-reflection, with transcribed dreams and extracts from books she is reading. Despite all this effort, we are floundering in the dark.

I confess I have come to dread these sessions. Unusually aware of the clock counting down the hour, I feel heavy and tired. The temptation to switch off is overwhelming. I am at a loss to account for this deadening feeling. Turning away from the narrative of a dream Anita is sharing today, I begin to tune in to my felt sense. Perhaps here I might discover the source of this disturbance in me. To my surprise I discover I cannot feel anything much, except a kind of deep exhaustion. Despite the richness of content in our session I feel quite numb. Senseless. It's an icy feeling, as though I find myself hardening through being left out in the cold. This nub of coldness is in me, but I sense it does not come from me. It seems to blow into the room the minute Anita steps through the door.

Each week Anita spills out her week's story, her reflections, her insights. She shows no interest in how they land with me. Preoccupied with her own revelation, she is largely unaware of my tender presence. I am a detail in the distance. That's all. Sensing my numbness, I begin to wonder if our sessions have become hard for me to bear because a part of me feels 'frozen out'. That's when it strikes me. I feel unseen. I find myself recoiling in shame. *I shouldn't need to be seen*, I tell myself. *These are Anita's sessions. My role is to see her.* Over the next few weeks I work hard to stay awake to my conflicted feelings of longing and self-censure. Soothing the shame of my need to be seen, I feel my frozen numbness begin to thaw. Something new begins to move within me. It is a deep ebb of loneliness.

Pausing the flow of Anita's reflections one day, I share how I'm feeling. I tell her a part of me feels 'left out in the cold'. I explain that this part feels young, lost and very lonely. 'She's on the verge of giving up,' I say. 'I am speaking now, interrupting our session, because I don't want her to give up. I want to bring this child into the warmth of our attention.'

In the ensuing silence Anita looks surprised, as though I have materialised out of nowhere. For once she is speechless. She draws in a large breath and holds it there. Her hand darts out in front of her, signalling to me to stop talking. Then, closing her eyes, she exhales long and slow, as if she has been holding her breath for years. With her eyes still closed, Anita nods. Her face flushes with the force of life returning. With this simplest of gestures I sense that we are both present to one another, perhaps for the first time.

For a brief moment Anita allows herself to feel the warmth of my care on her face, the ground of my presence beneath her feet. This intimacy of encounter is hard to bear. A trickle of feeling threatens to become a flood. She quickly returns to the safety of her self-sufficient world and resumes her telling of a dream. But a flicker of hope has been kindled.

Anita has dared to breathe. And in this space between words she has risked a moment of contact with me, and more importantly, with herself. The session marks the beginning of a thaw. This intake of breath and slow exhalation tell us more about her wounding and survival than all of her bulging notebooks. For where there is breath, there is life. And of course where there is life, there is also feeling. It seems that Anita has been holding her loneliness at bay by filling the space between us with words, compressing life, breath, and feeling into a hairline crack. No wonder I have been feeling so tired.

*

Psychotherapy is part of an oral tradition of storytelling as old as the hills. Its words are essentially spoken. They emerge from a living and vital presence, embodied with breath. The uncurated truth often gives itself away in moments when the breath-lines change. Speech may speed up or slow down. Sometimes words simply run dry and breath is all that remains. Then there are moments when the flow of speech is interrupted by a sharp shudder. A silent gasp. A sigh. A sob. Each of these shifts in breath bears witness to a change in the direction of the animating winds of being.

Recognising the breathlessness that deadens my sessions with Anita, I recall a poem by the great African-American poet Etheridge Knight. Knight describes the spoken word as 'a living organism' animated by how we breathe and defined by speech patterns shaped by our physical and emotional environment. He reminds us that 'the spoken word is a physical entity... As I'm talking to you, bones are moving in your inner ears. I'm physically touching you with my voice.'[51] It's the sound of speech that evokes feeling. Listening beyond the literal meaning of words we tune in to nuance, colouring and tone. That's how we are touched.

Born in Mississippi, Knight came to poetry from the oral tradition of the street, through toasts and rap. He first began to define himself as a poet in Indiana State Prison where he was serving an eight-year sentence for robbery. During these years he noticed that 'people who live in tight spaces take in the air differently than people who live in wide open spaces.'[52] His poem 'He Sees Through Stone', about a fellow inmate, offers us a powerful example of this compression. A recurring hiss sound seeps through the lines like air pressed out slowly from this incarcerated life. Spoken aloud, the poem's impact is visceral. Denied the oxygen of punctuation, the poem leaves me breathless.

We tend to think of our inner life as immaterial and invisible, a subtle dimension, more mind than matter, that lies beyond the reach of our senses. It can be helpful to remember that the word 'psyche' originates in the Greek noun *psukhé*, meaning 'breath', and on the verb *psykhein*, meaning 'to blow'. The 'immaterial substance' of our inner life blows through us and between us. Like the wind, which we discern through the rustle of leaves, or the ripple of water, psyche is revealed through the ways in which it touches and moves us. We register these invisible currents through that most subtle of sensory organs, the 'felt sense'. Beyond the more obvious gusts, there are times when we experience this interfusion as a mere tremble, a passing shudder, a slight chill in the air.

Like Martha Graham and Etheridge Knight, I too am on the lookout for movements in the ebb and flow of breath. To look for the living presence within words is an act of will. My mind is quick to seek out meaning in the words themselves and I lose sight of the animating ebb and flow, the 'physical entity' of speech. When I do manage to release myself from the narrative and just listen to the punctuations of air, I begin to get a sense of how the breath-lines fall when a truth is being spoken or when a truth is being strangled. This is intimate work. In fact it's hard to imagine a more intimate enquiry than one which tracks the very breath of life.

*

Seeing one another intimately, we must stay tuned to the ebb and flow of consent, a fragile interplay of trust that is never sealed. We engage in an intricate dance that honours the right to refuse disclosure, to evade, elude and retreat.

In his poem 'The Snakes of September', poet Stanley Kunitz writes about the shyness of snakes moving imperceptibly in his garden in the heat of summer. Long before he sees them, he senses their presence from their 'rustling', 'outracing' and 'pulsing'. Both snake and gardener begin their interplay of perception by allowing themselves to be touched by the subtle movements of a concealed presence:

> … as much as I responded to the garden, the garden,
> in turn responded to my touch, my presence.[53]

In September, when the nights become cooler, the snakes come out of hiding. His patient and reverent waiting is rewarded and he is finally able to touch them, first with his eyes and then with his hand:

> I put out my hand and stroke
> the fine, dry grit of their skins.
> After all,
> we are partners in this land,
> co-signers of a covenant.
> At my touch the wild
> braid of creation
> trembles.[54]

Reflecting on nearly a century of tending his garden Kunitz reminds us that seeing is an interplay in which we are 'co-signers of a covenant'. The snakes will not come out into the open to be touched unless they feel safe to do so. Without their consent Kunitz cannot see them. The fundamental point here is that *it is the subject seen who allows the disclosure.*

The concealed subject is both secret and sacred. To be seen is to allow the sacred to be disclosed. To push through this concealment would be an act of desecration. This same covenant shapes seeing within human encounter. Held in the eyes of the beholder the protective camouflage of our personality is parted, like the leaves in Kunitz' garden. We are laid bare.

This essential covenant of perception is most beautifully illustrated in another tale of human contact with the natural world, the true story of 'The Elephant Whisperer'.[55] In 1999 South African conservationist Lawrence Anthony was asked to give shelter to a herd of young elephants who had been traumatised by seeing members of their herd butchered by poachers. When they first arrived on his Thula Thula reserve the elephants were wild with grief. No one could get close to them. They broke out of their enclosure and wandered back into the bush. Determined to restore their faith in human contact, Lawrence left his home and went to live in the wilds. He stayed near them, gently murmuring his presence, occasionally singing to them. At first the elephants were unsettled and aggressive. Their eyes had seen too much. They no longer consented to see humans, nor to be seen by them.

Lawrence knew he would have to earn the elephants' trust. Intuitively he understood the two principles that lie at the heart of the covenant of trust. Firstly, he came to the place where the broken animals were. He left his own home and took up residence in theirs. Immersed in an untamed wilderness, he began to see as they saw. Away from the domesticated human world, ancient instincts began to awaken. He felt his senses sharpen and the life around him seemed to 'thrum at a richer tempo'. Secondly, Lawrence tuned in to the pace of the elephants. He recognised that elephants prefer slow, deliberate movements, so he ambled across, 'ostentatiously stopping to pluck a grass stem and pausing to inspect a tree stump', clearly taking his time.

Week after week Lawrence repeated his tender ritual. One day he moved closer to the herd. Something in the gaze he shared with the matriarch Nana suggested a new consent:

*Her soft eyes pulled me in. Then, almost in slow motion, I saw her gently reach out to me with her trunk*[56].

With her infinitely gentle gesture, it seemed the elephant and the man had arrived at an understanding, a fragile consent. Following the matriarch's lead the other elephants began to tolerate his presence. In the months that followed, a pattern evolved. The herd would occasionally turn up at his home and spend some time with him, before retreating again into the concealment of the bush. The elephants were always in charge of their own disclosure.

This extraordinary covenant remained unbroken up to, and beyond, Lawrence's death in 2012. A few days after his fatal heart attack the elephants made their way through the pristine Zululand bush to Lawrence's home. For two days they held vigil, perhaps honouring the sense that they were indeed 'partners in this land'. This ritual was repeated a year later, on the precise anniversary of his death.

Reflecting on this extraordinary covenant, Lawrence's wife Françoise commented that the elephants had taught them 'trust is not a given or a right, but it is hard earned over time'.[57]

*

In the weeks that follow Anita's brief moment of disclosure, I find myself remembering the story of the elephant whisperer. Like Nana's trunk reaching through the fence, our first moment of contact is fleeting and quickly followed by renewed concealment. This evolves into a tender game of hide and seek.

Anita offers me a puzzle of incomplete facts about herself, deliberately omitting the connecting pieces, making it almost impossible to join the dots. Or she floods the space with elaborate stories, often interrupting her own narrative, darting in a kind of zigzag pattern across my line of sight like a hare escaping capture. Anita does not consent to be seen at first. I have to meet her where she is, to move at her pace. Like the elephants, she needs me to tune into her rhythms of contact, to approach her slowly, letting her know that I am prepared to wait for her to consent to being seen by me. It is slow and patient work.

Anita's need for concealment reminds me that whilst all of us long to be seen deeply, many arrive wounded by the disregard of others. Where visibility is originally a shaming or unsafe experience, concealment can be life-saving. We bury more than our waste. More than our brokenness. We bury our treasure.

As she begins to open, to herself and to me, I look for evidence of Anita's consent in my own felt responses in the moment. An internal contraction signals that I may have come too close, or moved too fast. I may have to pause, change pace or direction. At first it is hard to catch the micro shifts of consent. When I overstep the mark, she vanishes back into renewed concealment. These moments of retreat are pregnant with significance. Secrecy often signals that we are approaching something significant, perhaps even something sacred. In time I begin to read the pattern. I notice that whenever my seeing is in danger of becoming too much for her, she deflects my enquiry with a tangential story. To build trust between us it is important to allow this deflection, but gradually I shorten the time it takes for me to return the focus to our interaction in the moment. Touched by this respect for her concealment, Anita allows herself to pause for breath more often. In these clearings the frozen feelings begin to thaw. Putting aside the notebooks, she begins to include the forsaken child.

Anita was just three when her baby brother arrived. George was a wonderful addition to the family. A fascinating creature with fat cheeks and tiny hands. He slept through the night and lay quietly rocking himself from side to side in his cot for hours. 'He's a good baby,' her mother reflected. As he reached his first birthday, Anita was dimly aware that her mother's warmth and affection gave way to a fretful preoccupation. She became distracted and short tempered. Mummy kept saying 'Not now darling!' and 'Shhhh!' A year later it was clear that something had changed. There were whispered conversations and visits to the doctor. What Anita didn't know, because no one spoke to her about it until much later, was that George had been born with a rare genetic disorder. He required round the clock care.

Increasingly Anita's mother, father and younger brother seemed to form a separate unit, a sub-family immersed in something intense and important. Occasionally, her mother would swoop in with a brief flash of attention. Out of nowhere she might ask 'Have you done your homework?' or 'What do you want for supper?' These sudden moments of visibility always felt searing and sharp against the frost of general disregard.

Frozen out of her mother's affection, Anita hardened her heart. Recognising her mother's fragility, the little girl cauterized her own feelings. Tucking the frozen child out of view, she decided she would feel nothing and need no one. Digging deep into her small self, she became a 'good girl' who always tried hard. Encapsulated in a world of her own, Anita ceased to expect anything from others. Fearful of scrutiny, she grew up with a painful ambivalence around being seen at all.

Unable to articulate the child's experience, to herself or to me, Anita's psyche impregnated me with her original experience. Like the forsaken child, I encountered the icy hand of invisibility. I too felt ashamed of my need to be seen. I too found myself hardening against the pain of loneliness. Through the invisible pathways of an 'interfusing thought', Anita conceived in me a lived experience of being 'frozen out'. She put the nub of cold inside me.

*

Before it is anything else, seeing is an experience of contact. Though sight and speech travel beyond the body, they still have the power to shape, hold and soothe. The touch of sight can also cut, scorch and excite. Seeing one another deeply, our perception is constantly sensing the tolerance of both seer and seen to the intimacy of opening. Careless or wilful scrutiny risks transgression. The word 'scrutiny' originates in the Indo-European root *sker* meaning to 'cut, cleave or hew' (*sker* also gives us the root for 'screw'). There is violence in it.

Working with tools to cut into wood and stone, British sculptor Barbara Hepworth understood that her hands could both transmit the shaping of her artistic intention and receive subtle signals relaying her material's response. She sensed when the touch of her tools risked cracking the stone or splintering wood. Where her right hand held the hammer firmly to articulate her vision, her left hand needed to be relaxed and sensitive, to pick up traces of the imminent and the emergent. She described her left hand as her 'listening hand':

*It listens… for the possibility or imminence of fractures.*[58]

As a sculptor, Hepworth placed great significance on the human hand. For her it was a symbol of the principle of touching and being touched which infuses all the senses. This correlation between seeing and touching is evident in her hospital drawings of 1947–1949. She made these drawings from life, having sat in on operations at an Exeter hospital when her daughter was hospitalised with a bone infection in 1944. In these exquisitely

81

observed drawings her focus rests on the tender interplay of the surgeons' eyes and hands.

In therapy we too are on the lookout for the possibility or imminence of fractures. Though the boundaries of intimacy preclude tactile contact, we sense the presence of the other. Like Hepworth we feel our way around 'rhythms of thought'. We touch (and are touched) through our seeing.

*

The principle of a tender vision is also articulated by painter Paul Cézanne, who advocated that the artist must be able to perceive through reading the 'two parallel texts' of nature. 'Nature seen and nature felt.' Cézanne likened the sensitivity of the artist to a photographic plate:

> … many skilful baths have brought this plate to the point of receptivity where it can be impregnated with the conscientious image of objects. Long labour, meditation, study, suffering, joy, and life have prepared it.[59]

The human 'receptive plate' is perhaps like the stretched skin of a drum made tender by a life of contact. Our word 'tender' is rooted in the Latin *tendere*, which means to 'stretch towards'. The idea of tenderness derives from the sense that something stretched becomes thin and so more vulnerable to the impressions of touch. From the Latin stem *tendere,* we also find the word *tendril,* the fingertip of a plant's shoot that stretches towards light, or the nib of a root which senses its way towards water. The sensitivity of these natural processes regulates just how much light or water the plant can tolerate. The tendril stretches in a sequence of micro movements towards essential life forces. It does not drive in a straight line towards light and water, but will pause, and turn to ensure the plant is neither starved nor flooded. The tracery of a winter tree is the imprint of all these minute organic choice points when the tendril regulated its contact with the 'otherness' of light, water and air.

Understood in this way, tender vision is essentially about *stretching out* beyond my own pre-conceptions and leaning towards the place where you are. It is about allowing myself to become *vulnerable* so I might be *touched* by the vital life force in you.

Through the tender interplay of opening and closing to my sight, Anita gradually emerges from her own disregard. We become partners in this disclosure. In one of her final sessions she shares this telling dream:

*I find myself in a shop full of old furniture and curiosities. Suddenly the door bursts open and a woman walks in. She has come looking for Victorian china. Spotting a teapot, she grabs it, buys it and leaves. Beyond this purchase all she sees is a collection of junk. Another woman enters. She pauses for a moment to take in the distinctive feel of this intimate little space. She nods to me and gestures to the interior (as though seeking permission to enter). Her eyes travel from object to object, her curiosity alive and her attention relaxed and open. An old clock with intricate engraving catches her attention, then a painted Russian Babushka doll. In a forgotten corner she discovers a basket of discarded textiles – silks, velvets and linen. In the dim light their textures are soft to touch. Holding them up she is careful not to drop anything. She places each object back as she found it.*

'What does the second woman see?' I ask. Allowing her eyes to rest in mine, Anita replies simply, 'Treasure'.

\*

Seeing through the living eye is intimate work. Kunitz suggests 'it's like someone removing a garment slowly, slowly.' This gradual process of revelation 'means getting down to the very tissue of experience.'[60] If we are to open in this way, we need to feel safe. This safety is built on a covenant of trust that is built over time in the intimate space between two people. Respect for what is secret is at the heart of this covenant. So much of contemporary human encounter fails to honour concealment. Hungry for instant disclosure, we put it all out there. Every life story is cloaked in layers of seclusion. Like poets and gardeners, we must be willing to discover the intimate complexity of the human landscape gradually, tenderly. What has been secret, what is most sacred, is revealed through a tender vision. Seeing in this way, we become instruments through which 'the braid of creation trembles.'

# PART TWO

# THE EYE OF DISCERNMENT

*Discerning:*
*from Latin dis = 'apart' + cerne = 'to separate'*

To distinguish a particular feature or moment
from within the subtle and fluid realms
of ambiguous, obscure, or immanent experience.

# CHAPTER SIX

# A SEEING PLACE

*'The sealed chamber'*

*We go to the theatre to have a communion with the truth of our existence, and, ideally, we leave it knowing that that kind of communion is still possible.*[61]

Sanford Meisner

Straddling the borders of West Virginia and Maryland lies an area known as 'The Quiet Zone'. Encircled by mountains and forests, 13,000 square miles of land lie silent beneath radio-quiet skies. Inhabitants in the small town of Green Bank live without microwaves or Wi-Fi and with limited mobile phone services. All radio transmission is restricted. This is not the edict of a modernity-rejecting faith community, but a regulation set down by the National Radio Astronomy Observatory to provide the ideal conditions for the operation of the world's largest steerable radio telescope.

The Green Bank Telescope's giant 2.3 acre dish is super sensitive. Within the sealed space of the Quiet Zone this enormous receptor can register the energy emitted by a single snowflake hitting the ground. It can track the radio signal emitted by activity in the solar system 13 billion years ago. Shielded from the chatter of modern life, it is able to focus on individual radio waves from deepest space and to track the infinitesimally faint clouds of hydrogen that hang out between the stars. Hydrogen is the building block of the universe, so discerning meaningful patterns within these cloudy gatherings and where they are heading are crucial clues to piecing together the history and future of our galaxy.

The sensitivity of the Green Bank Telescope, its opening onto the distant wonders of our universe, is secured within a sealed space. We too see ourselves and each other through opening. We open our senses, looking, listening, touching. We open our minds through imagination and ideas. We open our hearts to wonder and to love. Through the power of our sensitivity we are capable of tapping into frequencies that tell of stories constellated many generations ago. We can map human solar systems and so place each life within its own sphere of influence and significance. Opening our apertures wide, we discover that there are universes within each of us every bit as marvellous as those registered by the Green Bank Telescope.

Opening our seeing means allowing ourselves to become *vulnerable* to experience. Without vulnerability, as Brené Brown reminds us, there is no clarity of vision:

> *Vulnerability is the birthplace of love, belonging, joy, courage, empathy and creativity. It is the source of hope, empathy, accountability and authenticity. If we want greater clarity or deeper and more meaningful spiritual lives, vulnerability is the path.*[62]

This brings us to the nub of the matter. Without protection, our human apertures dare not open wide. Out in the un-encompassed world, we risk becoming flooded and over exposed. This is ever more so in a world where our sensitive human apprehension is under pressure from the innumerable shards of data, opinion and spin which assault our senses through digital media. Exposed to a chronic excess of stimulation in the compressed living of crowded urban spaces, we settle for the safety of seeing at a glance, through the narrow crack of the click and the swipe. Without opening, what we capture is increasingly crude and devoid of depth or significance. We become de-sensitised, to ourselves and to each other.

In the non-human world, sensitivity is power. We wonder at the marvels revealed to us through a technological perception that reaches out into the vastness of space and deep into the miniature worlds of microbiology and quantum mechanics. Billions of pounds are spent making these finely tuned instruments ever more sensitive. As technology becomes more sensitive, it seems that human beings risk becoming coarser. Spellbound by our need to be seen and trapped in our fear of missing out, we struggle to cut our umbilical connections with the infinitely distracting modern world. Set against the value system of our un-encompassed culture, enclosure can register as limitation, or even incarceration. To be shielded from the public gaze has become a sign of social failure. Subject to the ratcheting pressures of our increasingly complex world, we protect ourselves by becoming calcified and calloused. Armoured to the hilt, we increasingly forget that human beings are also instruments of perception. Resisting the option to switch off, to shut the door, we forgo the practice of seeing deeply.

If we are to open the aperture of perception we need a protected space that can shelter us from the storm. The early desert peoples of the Middle East understood the fundamental importance of enclosure. Our word *paradise* originally meant 'walled area'. In ancient Persian the word derives from *pairi* meaning 'around' and *daeza* meaning 'wall'. Originally these enclosed spaces served to shut out the harsh environment of the desert and create shelter for cultivation. Irrigated by running water, a most precious commodity in desert lands, the Persian gardens gave protection to a profusion of plants and flowers. Streams crossed at various points articulating the gardens into separate spaces. Patterns were formed and discreet areas defined. This organised containment allowed for the undifferentiated wilderness to find meaningful form.

From the Persian *pairidaezas* we get the idea of the walled garden as a nursery space where new life can take root, develop and grow. The Greeks borrowed the ancient Persian term and used it as *paradises*, meaning a 'heavenly place'. Significantly the biblical tradition reminds us that in time we must leave the garden, just as we must leave the womb (and the therapy relationship), when the time comes to make our way in the world.

Poet and gardener Stanley Kunitz explains how the enclosed space allows for the cultivation and articulation of vision:

> *In a sense, all creativity is a process of giving meaning to what is on a universal scale meaningless. The plant and the poet and the gardener collect these disparate, disorganized raindrops, sunrays, passing birds, and make something formal.*[63]

Perhaps, through our preoccupation with gaining exposure, we have forgotten the value of containment.

*

The walled nursery space of therapy allows our attention to become undivided, undiluted and undisturbed. In this shielded space it becomes possible to pick up traces of life and nuances of experience that simply do not register when competing on the crowded airwaves of ordinary encounter. Layers of feeling, memory and thought which are eclipsed in a busier, brighter environment become evident in this dimmed light and can be cultivated without fear of intrusion. Protected from ill winds and inundation, we begin to articulate our vision, to find meaning in what we see. We begin to discern more of what makes us human – a finely nuanced emotional palette and a deep sensibility.

At the threshold of each therapy meeting, the ubiquitous mobile phone is switched off. The fading of the little blue light signals a ritual sealing, which takes place psychologically as well as physically. The familiar reciprocity of relating is suspended and a spotlight falls on the intricate, complex and particular world of a single person. This is of great importance to human wellbeing, for to exist as a blend, blur, or smudge, is to settle for a life without articulation or significance.

Make no mistake, seeing deeply is hard work. Unlike our technological cousins, human receptors tire, weaken and flood easily. We are not designed to expose the cross-section of our hearts indefinitely. Like light-sensitive photographic paper, we have an optimum length of exposure, beyond which the image is lost altogether. The firm frame of the therapeutic hour provides sheltering containment, which ensures that our tender layers are not overexposed. Through weekly encounters, the opening of the human aperture is extended in a way that respects the limits of human sensitivity. We open deeply because we know that our seeing is enclosed in a time-limited space.

Safeguarded by the bonds of confidentiality, what is seen in therapy remains in the closed space. This seal of confidence makes it possible to struggle and to stumble without shame. Away from the glare of curated perfection, we are safe to flounder and to fail. The protection of this nursery space also encourages us to explore and to challenge. Shielded from toxic comparison or envious attack, we are safe to encounter the treasure of our distinction, the wonders of our unfolding nature. It becomes possible to experiment with shining.

The importance of the sealed space has been brought into sharp relief in the wake of pandemic lockdown. Like most of us, my work shifted into virtual space. Abandoning the solid and resolute shelter of my practice room, my therapy encounters transferred to video calls. All at once the seal was cracked. Through half-closed doors of bedrooms and kitchens, cats and dogs sauntered in, husbands who just 'happened to be passing' brought in cups of tea, voices became hushed so flatmates could not hear. The undivided thread of attention was punctured by the ping of email messages arriving in unguarded inboxes, the postman's knock at the door, neighbours passing by the window.

No longer held in the sealed container, I felt the walls of my heart strain to hold open the silences and in-between spaces in which new life is seeded. Attention fractured and dispersed. In this breached space, I noticed a dilution, a distancing, a shallowing of vision.

*

It occurs to me that there are perhaps only three places remaining where the ubiquitous mobile phone is turned off – the therapy room, places of worship and the theatre. In their own way, each of these sealed spaces fosters a quality of perception that comes close to communion.

We are perhaps most familiar with the power of the sealed space to heighten our perceptive sensitivity from experiences of theatre. The word itself is rooted in the Greek 'theasthai', which means a 'seeing place' (from theōros, meaning 'spectator' and thea, meaning 'view'). The Greek goddess Theia was guardian of sight. She endowed gold, silver and gems with their brilliance and intrinsic value. Theia was the inspiration for theatre, which was conceived as a place that illuminates the obscure and makes ordinary life vivid.

In therapy, as in theatre, this is what matters. To illuminate the intrinsic value of ordinary human life. To make our experiences vivid and distinct. Sometimes I find myself asking which is more 'real', the insights and perceptions experienced 'on stage' in my therapy room, or the more familiar seeing in the wide-open world outside. Starved of undivided attention, the person we are on the outside often settles for a pale imitation of the vivid person we encounter in the concentrated light of attention which becomes possible in a sealed space.

Actors I work with confess that they feel most authentic and most fully evident on stage. This feels like a paradox because we crudely equate theatre with pretence, an 'act' where imaginary circumstances are played out. We imagine that the real person is the one off-stage, illuminated by the clear daylight of our 'real' world. We forget perhaps that it is often the undivided attention of a beholder which renders us vivid and particular, which allows us to shine. The theatre offers this to actors on stage because in this sealed space there are no distractions. In the auditorium the lights of the familiar world are dimmed. Within the darkness a spot of light encircles the figures on stage. Their presence and distinction are all the more acutely evident because of the darkness that surrounds them.

*

In his seminal training book *An Actor Prepares*, Russian theatre director Konstantin Stanislavski (1863–1938) encouraged his students to work with the idea of the limelight as a 'circle of attention', a space sealed by surrounding darkness. This circle serves to focus perceptive concentration:

> When you have a spot of light surrounded by darkness, all the objects inside of it draw your attention because everything outside it being invisible there is no attraction there.[64]

Held in the spotlight Stanislavski's students observed:

> ... in such a small space as in this circle you can use your concentrated attention to examine various objects in their most intricate details, and also to carry on more complicated activities, such as defining shades of feeling and thought.[65]

When asked to experiment with enlarging their circle of attention, they found that it became increasingly difficult to hold in view all the points of interest within the light:

> *... we could not take in everything at once, but had to examine the area bit by bit, object by object, each thing within the circle making an independent point.*[66]

Everything that is meaningful and alive exists in relationship. To encompass this relational space, we need a field of vision small enough to allow us to keep everything in view. When we can no longer hold multiple elements simultaneously in our field of vision, insight shatters. Our brains switch into a sequential mode of perception. Seeing in this way means that we can no longer hold multiple perspectives simultaneously and in context. We lose sight of the relationship *between* things. It is hard to overstate the importance of this loss of contextual vision.

At the heart of Stanislavski's vision lies the insight that the smaller the circle of attention, the more we can see all at once. This paradox is familiar to me as a photographer. Through a pinhole aperture the focus of light is so acute that the depth of field is almost infinite. To register this depth of vision, the camera needs to be entirely sealed, so that the light of the image in focus can register in the pitch black without diffusion.

Speaking about the original camera obscura (which means 'dark chamber'), Leonardo da Vinci expressed the wonder of this paradox:

> *Who would believe that so small a space could contain the images of all the universe?*[67]

*

94

Like the Green Bank Observatory, we can be listening stations for dimensions of original experience obscured or lost in time. We too are instruments of perception. Searching the vast open spaces within, we are looking for patterns and pathways that allow us to see critically into the intelligence of our human universe. We scan the internal firmament for signs of new beginnings, for the nativity happening this very minute.

To catch the birth of stars within us, we need to be alert to the music of the moment.

# CHAPTER SEVEN

# IN THE BLINK OF AN EYE

*Rachel's Story Part One ~ 'Caught red-handed'*

*Moments of recognition between composer and listener happen somehow like sitting in two passing trains. You only make out the person in the other train during a fleeting glance through a window.*[68]

Arvo Pärt

A shiny clingfilm of cheerfulness covers Rachel's face, denying air and movement to the being beneath. 'I've been bulimic since I was fourteen,' she tells me. Her voice is bright but brittle. It's as though she has just told me she has blue eyes and brown hair. Rachel is in her final year of a law degree. 'It's hard work,' she tells me, and then in a voice that sounds strained and off-key, she adds 'but very rewarding'. The expression on her face remains set. Nothing moves. Buried in the subtext of this first meeting I hear the silent plea 'find me'.

Our early sessions resound with stories about other people in Rachel's life. She returns often to accounts of her amazing parents, both barristers in a successful legal practice. Each week she brings a new drama from the courtroom to share with me. The more they unfold into their brilliance, the more eclipsed her life seems to become.

Everything needs to slow down so we can attend to what is happening in the currents of her own being. Nothing about this is easy. We are working against the grain of a lifetime's habit of tuning herself out. It's as though we are sitting by a mountain stream alive with surface burble and babble. I feel myself leaning in, searching for the lower octaves of a deeper sound, a basso continuo beneath these top notes. Estonian composer Arvo Pärt articulates the intention of deep listening like this:

> *The complex and many-faceted only confuses me... What is it, this one thing, and how do I find my way to it? Traces of this perfect thing appear in many guises – and everything that is unimportant falls away.*[69]

This 'one thing', it seems to me, is not some kind of ideal or general truth. It registers in the moment when something, or someone, is simply true to their original nature. Authentic. Intact. *Sound.*

'What is it that you listen for?' I ask a musician friend. Sipping mugs of Italian coffee, we are sitting at her kitchen table musing over the parallels between the musical conversations in her string quartet and the interplay of two people in a therapy relationship. 'Notes don't simply add up to something meaningful,' she says. 'When I play I'm listening for a deeper voice within the music. I'm feeling my way towards the sound as it was originally intended. Fresh. Sheer. And wholly uncorrupted.' 'And how do you know when you have found this original sound?' I ask. 'Mostly you just know when you haven't found it,' she replies. 'The musical conversation is always a kind of yearning or searching for something lost.' This strikes me as a perfect description of the therapy conversation. We listen for traces of the original, uncorrupted 'voice' of a person. The core of who they uniquely are. Life circumstances tend to bury or distort the 'soundness' of this indigenous self. We suffer this loss.

Away from the drama of other people's stories, Rachel seems lost. She covers this up with 'complex and many-faceted' stories from outside of her own experience. In the riverbed of her being there is no comforting sound. Just a dull and desolate silence.

Pianist and conductor Daniel Barenboim suggests that in music there are several types of silence:

*There is a silence before the note, there is a silence at the end and there is a silence in the middle.*[70]

Within the therapy conversation there is always 'the silence in the middle'. For every word spoken there is, at the same time, all that is unspoken. There is all that remains unspeakable. Silence can be the blueprint to a life. It has a history, a form. Silence is a presence, an 'unthought known' drawn from the inchoate depth of being. Sometimes we have no words to clothe this 'known' because the buried experience is rooted in an age before we developed speech. Then there are silenced truths that are simply unspeakable, due to shame or terror. Or love. Or loss. At their deepest our truths are simply ineffable, too great to be expressed in words.

'What then do we "do" with this silence?' Arvo Pärt was once asked by a conductor during rehearsals. Pärt replied, 'You don't do anything. You wait. God does it.'

In the West we have come to understand silence as absence, nothingness, void. We fear it greatly. Eastern traditions on the other hand have always emphasised the dynamic relationship between silence and sound. Japanese Zen Buddhism celebrates the idea of 'ma' as the unsounded realm that gives birth to all things. Composers like Tōru Takemitsu call this 'liminal silence', an initiating realm at the threshold of all expression. This 'ma' is not a void, but an entity, filled with energy and purpose. Musicians experience 'ma' on the upbeat that heralds a new phrase and in the breath before the first note of a song.

Listening for this first note, Rachel and I will have to hold an unbroken line of attention. We cannot afford to miss a beat, because sometimes within the familiar rhythms of conversation, there is a shift of moment, a tear in the surface score, which acts as a portal to a buried truth. These shifts are often fleeting, like a passing shard of light, or shy like a child in need of coaxing. Tender truths, Stanislavski reminded his drama students, 'do not make their appearance on the stage in the way you think… They flash out in short episodes, individual moments.'[71] To catch them, we must stay tuned, moment by moment, to the interplay between us.

Building on Stanislavski's vision, Sanford Meisner rooted each action on stage in an instinctive *response* to a change of moment between two actors. He encouraged his students to focus on the subtle rhythms of *interaction*.

Meisner drew on two core principles, which I have found to be equally important in the interplay of therapy:

1. *Don't do anything unless something happens to make you do it.*
2. *What you do doesn't depend on you; it depends on the other fellow.*[72]

Instead of 'figuring out' what to do, Meisner's students were encouraged to notice and respond to shifts of emotion and thought given away moment to moment in the gestures and intonations of other members of the cast. These shifts, he proposed, signal the emergence of something vital and authentic in the interplay.

In my experience as a psychotherapist, revelation also happens through the creative interplay between people. Through a dynamic of 'call and response' we listen out for the margin of concord, or the degree of dissonance, which expresses itself in the interplay. Small changes of expression, posture and tone suggest when we are in tune and when we are off key. Each articulation is like a musical phrase, which is our best sounding of an original truth.

*

Like actors and musicians, psychotherapists start by following a given score – a particular methodology or modality. They sight-read note for note. But as they mature their aim needs to be to move beyond this text. Freed from the rigid lines of concept and technique, they listen out for the more subtle frequencies of unscripted experience that sound in the creative space between two people. The vitality of this interplay relies fundamentally on the responsiveness of the individuals, on their ability to listen to one another in the moment.

Unshackled from formulaic methodology, psychotherapy is 'live performance'. At its best it achieves the kind of spontaneity that is the hallmark of jazz improvisation. In the liner notes to the seminal jazz album 'Kind of Blue' by Miles Davis, Bill Evans outlined the way in which the legendary trumpet player conceived his pieces. Miles arrived at the recording studio with 'sketches', some chord progressions perhaps, which indicated to the group an outline for what was to be played. The sketches, he recalls, were 'exquisite in their simplicity' and yet they contained 'all that is necessary to stimulate performance with the sure reference to the primary conception.'[73] Within the frame of these sketches, Miles trusted in the live interactions of musicians playing off each other. The group had never played these pieces prior to the recordings, yet the first complete performance of each was a take.

The conceptual frameworks through which we see one another also need to be lightly held. Sketches rather than scores. If the script we play from is too rigid, if the theory is formulaic, then the interplay will rest on it like an old scaffold. Our listening will slump, our attention drift. We will miss the moment of revelation. Perhaps it is the musicians and poets of the street, the jazz musicians and the rappers, with their live improvisation, who understand most instinctively the risks we must take to seize the emergent truth of the moment.

In therapy, weeks of interplay often turn on a decisive moment when the rhythm of interplay suddenly breaks or turns. It might jar or snag, plummet or soar. A creative rupture punctures the flow with a change of pitch or key, a sudden silence or a pregnant pause. (Jake's story in chapter two described one such moment.) Something fresh, un-curated and authentic can enter the space at any moment.

*

Sitting with Rachel, neither of us can be sure what we are listening for. There is no score. All I know at this point is that this opening onto the buried text will surface in a kind of rupture, in a moment of unscripted discord. In a sudden change of key.

Rachel arrives at her session today flushed and flustered. Her father has just won a high profile legal case. 'You must feel very proud,' I venture. 'I am,' she replies. As she says this, Rachel's hand jerks suddenly towards her throat, which flushes red. She coughs, as though choking on her own words. A look of bewilderment flashes across her face. The whole gesture flashes past us in the blink of an eye.

There is a sharp discrepancy between the story Rachel is telling me and the evidence of her body, which seems to be saying something else entirely. The intensity of feeling that accompanies this moment of unbidden disclosure comes as a shock. We are both suddenly wide-eyed and silent.

When a personal truth sounds within human experience, it is unmistakable. Virginia Woolf refers to these encounters with truth as 'moments of being' which interrupt 'the rapid passage of events and actions.' These fissures in the surface stream of our habitual lives register as 'single and solemn moments of concentrated emotion.'[74] They strike us in the most unexpected and ordinary of circumstances and offer, Woolf suggests, a glimpse of 'something real behind appearances', a pattern hidden within the cotton wool of our distracted lives. Rarely revelations of mythic proportions, they are 'little daily miracles, illuminations, matches struck unexpectedly in the dark'.[75]

In the heat of this moment with Rachel, I find myself blushing, as though unaccountably shy in the presence of something 'other'. I am aware of a break in eye contact and a temporary cessation in my ability to think. Poet Rainer Maria Rilke speaks of this moment of disclosure:

> *The moment when something new has entered us, something unknown; our feelings grow mute in shy embarrassment, everything in us withdraws, a silence arises, and the new experience, which no one knows, stands in the midst of it all and says nothing.*[76]

In this heightened moment I am left with the sense that Rachel has just given herself away. She has been 'caught red-handed'. The discord between her words and her actions seems to indicate that we have come close to a place of fracture, or revelation. Perhaps Rachel has stumbled into the dwelling place of a forbidden truth. Maybe an unbearable memory has finally found its voice. It seems we have found a hairline crack in the surface narrative, a way through to the vital subtext. Through this opening we glimpse a fleeting view of a place beyond our knowing. Something, or rather someone, has just broken through the clingfilm.

Faced with this flash of disclosure, there needs to be a decisive act of commitment, of capture. Surrendering everything else, we must step forward to seize the moment.

*

Photographer Henri Cartier-Bresson famously coined the term 'the decisive moment' as the title of his 1952 book. This unassuming Frenchman pioneered the art of street photography and inspired a whole new genre of photojournalism. Armed with his handheld Leica, Cartier-Bresson sought to capture fleeting moments of significance in the relationships between people. His images are not the product of elaborate preconception or clever post production (he preferred not to edit or crop his images). With a few rolls of 35mm film in his pocket he simply walked around and allowed himself to absorb the fullness of his subjects, until he sensed a decisive moment.

In his early pictures he concentrated on street people, on gipsies, children and prostitutes. Through his lens, he captured fleeting gestures and glances, split second correlations of form and feeling. His ability to capture complex moments of relationship in the blink of an eye made him one of the great photographers of the twentieth century.

Cartier-Bresson described his camera as 'an instrument of intuition and spontaneity' through which the photographer 'questions and decides simultaneously'.[77] His images remind us that in our seeing, we are not only concerned with breath and comprehensiveness of vision. We are on the lookout for *significance*:

> To me, photography is a simultaneous recognition, in a fraction
> of a second, of the significance of an event as well as of the precise
> organisation of forms that give it proper expression.[78]

With a sensitivity comparable to that of a musician, Cartier-Bresson searched for a particular resonance of truth, or beauty. He was quite simply a master of discernment. Critics keen to learn the secrets of his art repeatedly asked about his equipment and technique. With fierce simplicity he would reply 'I know when to shoot – that's all'.[79]

> Sometimes you have a feeling that here are all the makings of a
> picture – except for one thing that seems to be missing. But what

*one thing? Perhaps someone suddenly walks into your range of view. You follow his progress through the viewfinder. You wait and wait, and then you finally press the button – and you depart with the feeling (though you don't know why) that you've really got something.*[80]

Suspended in the 'decisive moment' of Rachel's unguarded disclosure, I too am left with the feeling (though I don't know why) that we've 'really got something'. Somewhere in the margins of my line of sight, I catch a glimpse of a half-buried fragment. It fleets into my awareness. A random shape beyond recognition. This blink of awareness is reminiscent of that moment when we wake with the tail-end of a dream already disappearing under the bright light of our waking consciousness.

Faced with an anomaly, the urge to stay with the known can be enormous. The well-trodden pathways of our minds are quick to dismiss the unfamiliar as nonsense, marginal or irrelevant. It's probably nothing, I hear myself thinking. I face a split-second choice. If I interrupt Rachel's narrative, she may lose her thread. If I don't, we will miss the opportunity to explore the significance of her curious gesture. There's a risk either way.

*

This moment of commitment is beautifully demonstrated in the film *The Mystery of Picasso* made in 1956 by Henri-Georges Clouzot. Picasso is reputed to have said 'You don't make art. You find it.' In a live recording of the painter's creative process, this film shows us how he finds it. Drawing a reclining figure, Picasso begins by simply outlining one curve after another, making marks, covering the page. It's as though this is the start of a conversation – a call and response between himself and the marks. His conversation is intense, fluid, full of rapt attention. We get the feeling he's after

IN THE BLINK OF AN EYE

something particular, something that resonates with significance in the moment.

Suddenly Picasso seems to reach a kind of tipping point. He picks up the scent of something beginning to sound through all his mark-making. He is drawn to the way the woman's head rests on her hands. After this, everything else becomes unimportant. With an extraordinary directness we see him dip a thick brush into ink and paint over the exquisite lines he has just drawn. Most of the image is obliterated in a few bold strokes. Gone. All that remains is 'the one thing' which interests him. Alarmed at the erasure of the perfect drawing Clouzot asks 'Isn't that a risk?' to which Picasso replies, 'Risk is exactly what I'm going for.'

Watching this creative process, what is so liberating to see is how unattached Picasso is to his own artistry and technique. It's as though he scans his own marks, searching for a doorway through which the 'one thing', the kernel of the subject, can surface into the centre of his field of vision. Then he discards everything else. This act of surrender to something beyond preconception reminds us that in our search for significance, we must be willing to let go of everything. Discernment, it seems, rests in the art of subtraction.

*

Interrupting Rachel's glowing account of her father's legal triumph, I draw our attention to the dissonant movement of her hand to her throat. I mirror back to her what I have just seen. There is a subtle shift in our relating. The flow of time stops. Free from the time-worn script we enter virgin territory. Faced with this decisive moment, we let go of everything else.

Like an encryption, Rachel's gesture contains a vital truth that needs to be 'deciphered'. The word *decipher* originates in the old Arabic arithmetic symbol *sifr*, meaning 'zero'. Over time its meaning broadened to imply an absence or a 'nothing'. So, to *de-cipher* means 'to un-nothing' (a double negative meaning to 'find something'). Later, when numbers were used as substitutes for letters, the word *cipher* came to refer to an encryption, the concealment of a significant message within something commonplace, ordinary, unremarkable. To decipher the significance that lies encrypted within the everyday, we need to pull our attention away from the curated narrative and look into the discordant detail.

*

Speaking of revelation, thirteenth-century mystic Meister Eckhart wrote:

> *When the soul wants to experience something, she throws out an image in front of her and steps into it.*[81]

The image may take the form of a word, a sound or a gesture. Its significance is encoded. Rachel and I have stumbled on a door. Neither of us know what may lie beyond it. Maybe nothing. Holding the door open, we agree to step into it.

# CHAPTER EIGHT

# VIEWS OF THE INTERIOR

*Rachel's Story Part Two ~ 'Inside the Minotaur's house'*

*Revelation doesn't come easy. You have to fight for it. There is that*
*moment when you suddenly open a door and enter into the room*
*of the unspeakable. Then you know you're really speaking.*[82]

Stanley Kunitz

For many years I have been drawn to the intimate paintings of
Dutch artist Johannes Vermeer, best known for his painting 'Girl
with a Pearl Earring'. Breaking with the tradition of art depicting
heroic action and epic tragedy, Vermeer painted views of the
interior, domestic scenes where ordinary men and women are
deeply absorbed, making music or reading. The stillness that
surrounds these concentrated subjects draws the viewer's attention
to the interiority of their worlds. Light pours into the rooms they
occupy through windows and doors, saturating them with colour,
suggesting perhaps an inner illumination.

Visiting the Dutch collection at London's National Gallery a few
years ago, I caught a glimpse of a small five-sided box mounted on
a stand. It was unremarkable. Nothing to write home about. Still,
it piqued my curiosity. A closer inspection of the box revealed two
pinhole apertures, one on each opposing side. Peeping through
I found myself looking directly into a hall from which four open
doors afforded glimpses of further rooms. All at once the wider

gallery disappeared and I was drawn into the expansive and intricately articulated interior of a seventeenth-century Dutch house, complete with figures going about the ordinary activities of daily life. On a chair across the hall lay a woman's pearl necklace and comb. Through another open door, with a broom beside it, a woman sat reading, while a man peered at her through a window. Beyond him lay a vast unknown hinterland. From the opposite porthole I glimpsed a second woman in bed. She may or may not have been alone. A man's broad-rim hat with a shoulder-belt and sword hung by a nearby doorway, near which a spaniel sat waiting, expectantly.

As I cast my gaze across the scene, I found myself wondering: why is the woman in bed in broad daylight? Where is the man whose hat and sword hang on the wall? And what might the spaniel be waiting for?

'Peepshow with Views of the Interior of a Dutch House' is the most extraordinary surviving example of a 'perspective box'. Painted by Samuel van Hoogstraten, a contemporary of Vermeer, it uses a series of masterful distortions of perspective to achieve a complex illusion in which the inside of the box appears larger than the outside. The exterior of the box is unremarkable. Seen through the peepholes however, its interior is spacious, intriguing and remarkably beautiful.

*

The flat surface of everyday life is littered with doorways onto interior realms that reveal, through a series of openings, an intimate, expansive and vital world. Children quite naturally see in this way. They see through the recognisable surface. The most unremarkable fragment of experience becomes a keyhole, an opening onto an intricately articulated hinterland. Through their sense of possibility these interior realms become enormous. We have only to think of the rabbit hole in Alice in Wonderland or the wardrobe in C. S. Lewis' Narnia adventures to remember the revelatory powers of this portal vision.

The Lion the Witch and the Wardrobe opens with four children defying the boredom of a rainy day by exploring a forgotten corner of their uncle's rambling old house. They enter an unremarkable room, which looks quite empty, except for a large wardrobe:

> *There was nothing else in the room at all except a dead blue-bottle on the windowsill.*[83]

The older children, Edmund, Susan and Peter, have already begun to succumb to the flattening of adult perception. They glance over at the wardrobe door with eyes that are quick to move on, bored by the familiarity of its outer form. To them it is a wardrobe like all other wardrobes.

Significantly it is the youngest of the four children, Lucy, who stops to wonder:

> *She thought it would be worthwhile trying the door of the wardrobe, even though she felt almost sure that it would be locked. To her surprise it opened quite easily.*[84]

The revelation through the wardrobe begins with a suspension of dis-belief. Lucy's imagination is still vital. She trusts in the possibility of concealed worlds beyond the self-evident surface. She opens the wardrobe door and risks stepping into 'nothing'. All this takes is the thought that 'it would be worthwhile trying the door'. In this simple, decisive move, Lucy leaves the wider narrative and the other children behind. She steps into the wardrobe and rubs her face against the rows of fur coats within.

As she goes further in, the familiar limits of perception (first the door and then the rows of coats) gradually yield to a deeper reality. Holding her arms out in front of her, lest she bump into the back of the wardrobe, Lucy remains connected to the familiar world of recognisable forms. At the same time, she opens herself to the possibility of discovering something unknown. Pushing the soft folds of the coats aside she begins to think to herself, 'This must be a simply enormous wardrobe!'

*

In the split-second it takes to catch sight of the fleeting motion of Rachel's hand suddenly clutching her throat, I find myself thinking, It's probably nothing. At the same time another voice niggles within me. Like Lucy in the Narnia tales, I wonder if it would be worthwhile trying the door. Leaving the familiar narrative aside, Rachel and I agree to step into 'nothing'. This act of commitment takes courage, because like many of us, she has come to believe that behind the surface of her life, beyond the borrowed labels and the drama of other people's lives, there is just an empty space. It's as though she imagines opening a door onto her inner world, only to find a dead bluebottle on the windowsill.

This stepping into the unknown relies on the suspension of disbelief. It requires what the poet John Keats called 'Negative Capability':

> ... when a man is capable of being in uncertainties, mysteries, doubts, without any irritable reaching after facts and reason.[85]

Rachel struggles to articulate the obscure root of her gesture. 'It's not a new feeling,' she confesses, 'but I try to avoid it. I don't like the way it makes me feel.' Her eyes are suddenly hot with tears. The pull to turn away from this unwelcome feeling is palpable. I need to act quickly to get a foot in the door. Sensing the need to stay with the wisdom of the body, I ask Rachel how she might *enact* this dangerous feeling, if she gave it a free reign.

Rachel pauses, as though gathering courage to step into her image. Suddenly, with newfound conviction, she stands up, raises her right foot and brings it down heavily on the floor. Unnerved by the force of this stomping, every ounce of me strains to stay with the unfamiliar presence emerging. 'And what does your foot want to do?' I ask. Looking straight at me, Rachel replies, 'It wants to wreck things. Spoil things. Stamp on things.'

Released from its buried chamber, a newly untethered creature seems to have been set loose from the darkness. To my surprise I find myself punctured by an image of the Minotaur, the mythical creature described by Ovid as half-man, half-bull. Locked away in the bowels of a labyrinth the creature was severed from its natural sources of sustenance and fed on the unnatural offerings of sacrificed maidens and youths. Unhinged by this monstrous treatment, the Minotaur became crazed with grief. That's when I recall Rachel's 'bulimia' diagnosis. The word originates in the Greek bous, meaning 'bull' and limos meaning 'hunger'. Rachel is bull-hungry. She is also bull-angry.

Drawing on my own courage I ask 'What things would you wreck? What might you want to stamp on?' With a new-born confidence Rachel answers, 'All the beautiful, special, amazing things that everyone else gets to do, except me.' And there we have it, our first view onto the overlooked interior of her being. Peeping through the narrow crack of her incongruous gesture we now have a glimpse of a concealed drama full of choked-up longing, wrapped up in annihilating envy. Instead of a 'nothing', an 'emptiness', a 'zero', what we have stumbled on, beneath the clingfilm of compliance, is the forsaken cry for an unlived life.

Released from its desiccated authority, the label 'bulimia' comes alive as an idea through which a vital inner drama can be discerned. It is no longer a seal defining her surface symptom, but a window opening onto a hidden truth.

Instinctively we both know that this revelation is not the 'back of the wardrobe'. Like Lucy feeling her way through the rows of fur coats, we have to keep moving forward until we emerge into a clearing. To explore the roots of her hunger, I ask Rachel when she last felt deeply fulfilled. 'Not for a very long time' she replies. 'Not since I was a child.' She pauses, eyes bright with memory. 'Before she died, my grandmother gave me a dolls-house. A three-storey replica of a Georgian townhouse. I loved it more than anything.'

Tucked away in her bedroom with this handmade treasure, Rachel would spend hours, lost in an intimate world of imaginal play. The dolls-house occupied a large bay window in her bedroom. Many of the original pieces of furniture had been lost, so she would refashion everyday objects to replace them. Postage stamps became framed masterpieces on the walls, a small stack of matchboxes, brightly painted, stood in for a chest of drawers, whilst the dining table began life as a playing card glued onto a bobbin of cotton thread. Lost in the making of these miniature worlds she would feel enormous, like Alice in Wonderland.

To bring the dolls-house to life, I suggest that Rachel might like to make some drawings. Reaching for the coloured pens, she fills the paper with intricate detail. Released from the clingfilm, Rachel's face is rapt. When she eventually looks up, I ask if she still has the dolls-house. 'No,' she replies in a flat tone. 'Not since I started secondary school.'

On that crisp autumn day in her eleventh year, Rachel returned home to discover a smart black desk in the place where the dolls-house once stood. 'Dolls houses,' her father explained firmly, 'are for babies.' It was time for his daughter to grow up. Blind with a shame-filled grief Rachel searched everywhere for the dolls-house but found nothing. Her heart's true joy was never mentioned again.

Over the months that followed Rachel was repeatedly told to put away all her 'childish play'. Her parents had high hopes for her, they said. There was nothing to stop her making it all the way to the top. If she worked hard, she too could be a barrister one day. Rachel was rewarded for studying hard and for being helpful to her mother. She found herself increasingly walking in the shadow of other people's expectations. Sealed up with shame, the creative child was hidden away, like the minotaur, in a dark chamber deep inside.

Recalling this painful betrayal clearly for the first time, Rachel begins to sense the buried truth, which surfaced so unexpectedly as she recounted the news of her father's legal triumph. Lauding his achievement, she had caught herself in a flash of longing for her own joy, for the joy that he had so definitively trampled on. Horrified by the exposure of her envy and forbidden longing, the shamed child had reached towards her throat in an unsuccessful attempt to strangle the dangerous disclosure.

Staying with her body, I ask Rachel where she feels the wound of her lost joy. Placing her hand on her stomach, she replies 'Here,' and then with feeling she adds 'I feel barren.' The word pierces the space between us, with the resonant howl of original experience.

To decipher her word 'barren', Rachel and I draw up a list of antonyms.

*Barren (antonyms): fertile, fecund, cultivated, populated, replanted, fruitful, rich, lush, growing, productive.*

The use of antithesis is rather like using complementary colours in a painting. By placing red against a green, blue against orange, yellow against purple, the colour of experience becomes vivid, precise and particular. Looking at the opposite of 'barren' we find questions that point the way forward. What could it mean to cultivate the soil of her being? How might she populate her life with others who would support her creativity? Where might she look to find the seeds of a fruitful life? Guided by these questions, we begin to discern the way ahead.

Rachel needs to cultivate the soil of her being, to bear fruit. She needs to bear her own fruit. Our starting point is to mark out the boundary of her territory, to delineate what is hers from what is not hers.

Rachel's word 'barren' replaces the borrowed labels and opens a vital new doorway onto her interior. Through it she begins to see her suffering with new lucidity. She reconnects with the little girl whose particular gifts and longings were left unacknowledged and untended in the shadow of her parents' blinkered vision. Severed from her own truth, Rachel's soil has become clogged up with other people's dreams. Little wonder she has been gagging. Together we explore all the 'beautiful special amazing things' she had secretly loved as a child. We begin to breathe life into the longings that were suffocated under the blanket of her parents' blind will for her to follow in their footsteps.

The recovery of Rachel's original joy does not happen overnight. It takes time for her to trust in the forbidden truth of her gesture, to free herself from the injunctions inherited from her parents. This journey home centres on making her disavowed creativity and her longings vivid, distinct and legitimate. A tough few years lie ahead. The Minotaur refuses to resume its place in the shadows. Setting aside her legal studies, she makes room in her life for the bull-hunger and the bull-anger which have for so long laid buried. Recognising that she will not 'make it to the top' after all, Rachel confronts her father's crushing disappointment and her own residual shame.

Like Lucy in the The Lion, the Witch and the Wardrobe, Rachel begins to see a light ahead of her 'not a few inches away where the back of the wardrobe ought to have been. But a long way off.' Her essentially creative nature gradually reclaims its place at the centre of her life. In time she steps out into the light of her own Narnia. These days Rachel is a set designer for a children's theatre company. She creates spaces on stage for the play of imagination. The little girl with the dolls-house has finally grown up.

\*

I can still remember my first reading of The Lion, the Witch and the Wardrobe. I was nine years old. It felt as though a door had opened inside me – a door that I hadn't even known was there. It was thrilling. Stepping through similar portals over many years of therapy encounter, I have discovered all manner of concealed doorways opening onto intricately articulated interiors. These portals onto our inner worlds are generally very narrow. Like holes in sea ice, they open and close, allowing us only a brief window onto the ocean beneath. We must be decisive and courageous if we are to discover what lies beyond them.

In his account of diving in Antarctica, explorer and nature writer Barry Lopez captures the faith that underlies this moment of stepping into nothing. Describing the experience of dropping through a six-foot-deep hole in the ice, he writes:

> I cannot explain how I managed to do this. The draw for me was knowing that the world down there was brilliantly lit, rich with life and beautiful.[86]

If we are to see into the hidden wisdom of our hearts, we must be willing to enter the darkness of uncharted space. There we begin to decipher, to 'un-nothing', the vital depths of our original nature. Wilfred Bion reminds us that our attention becomes acute because of the absence of light:

> ... one must cast a beam of intense darkness so that something which has hitherto been observed by the glare of illumination can glitter all the more in the darkness.[87]

The Greek word for darkness is *skotos* and the ability to see in conditions of extreme low light is known as '*scotopic vision*'. This is the kind of night vision that picks up tiny traces of movement in the darkness of subterranean places. Severed from the light of the known, we learn to trust in a kind of night vision that draws us on through layer upon layer of revelation. In this twilight zone our powers of perception become attuned to nuance, slight of hand, detail and tone. We begin to see like moles. *Through* the dark.

Sometimes, if we're lucky, the earth moves.

# CHAPTER NINE

# THE LANGUAGE OF REVELATION

*Ella's story ~ 'The Shredding'*

*To see clearly is poetry, prophesy, and religion – all in one.*

John Ruskin[88]

As she walks through the door today Ella looks unsteady, as though the floor might start moving at any moment. She has survived the earthquake, but the danger of aftershocks is ever present. It's been six months since her husband's affair ripped through her world. Since then she has been fighting to keep her marriage alive. Hope and despair have wrestled in an unsightly brawl.

The stability of the chair brings some relief. Ella's breathing slows. Eyes pinned to the floor she says, 'He won't leave her. He's. Leaving. Me.' The last three words land heavily in the room with the deliberate tread of footsteps still reeling from a blow. Hearing the stark reality of her own disclosure, Ella looks suddenly quite lost. Powerful crosscurrents of emotion swell within her. They feel agitated, forbidding, pitiless. At the mercy of these blind forces, her inner world has suddenly become a terrifying and dangerous place. Immersed in feeling, Ella is at sea.

*

In the wildness of emergent experience, where new internal landscapes are forming, our emotions jostle together. They lie 'twisted about one another in giant and swollen groupings.'[89] It's genuinely difficult to tell them apart. At times like these, language is not an adornment. It's a navigational tool essential for survival. Words are harbours in the wild seas of original experience. Places of anchorage. Sheltered within their walls, we begin to see where we are.

Disturbed by the swell of emotions, language often seems to fail us. Everything withdraws into a tunnel of silence as we confront feelings that appear unspeakable. In fact, all original experience is by definition, unspoken. Each attempt to name what we feel, T. S. Eliot reminds us, is 'a raid on the inarticulate'.[90]

In the intimate mystery of revelation, the words we use really matter. Words render our emotions and thoughts apparent, vivid and differentiated. They are like dream catchers, conjuring experience into form, out of nothing. The language of revelation is rarely found in psychological glossaries. It is rooted in everyday words and figures of speech, in a poetic vernacular that was once commonplace.

Writing in the seventeenth century, the great Japanese haiku master Basho shows us that poetry is not just a way of writing about the world, it is a way of seeing it. Poetry unveils, it lays bare the surprising things around and within us which we might otherwise overlook. Basho's intimate visions remind us that poetry is the experience of seeing into the heart, the deep nature of something. This seeing through words need not be the province of an elite. It arises naturally in all of us when we become intimate with our subject:

*Your poetry issues of its own accord when you and the object have become one – when you have plunged deep enough into the object to see something like a hidden glimmering there.*[91]

Poets articulate this glimmering truth precisely because they stay with ineffable feelings long enough for language to emerge from the depth of the feeling itself. They bear with the experience of being tongue-tied. American poet and essayist Ralph Waldo Emerson reminds us that the birthing of articulate vision can test us to the core.

> *Stand there, balked and dumb, stuttering and stammering, hissed and hooted, stand and strive, until at last rage draw out of thee that dream-power which every night shows thee is thine own.*[92]

The point made so powerfully here is that for language to reveal our emotional worlds, the words used need to be 'thine own'. The fragile cargo of meaning born by our feelings is easily miscarried by the eager intervention of borrowed language. Budding insight becomes buried under the dead weight of dusty descriptors.

To locate herself in the still raw moment of her desolation Ella could reach for a phrase from the common lexicon of loss. She might say she feels 'heart-broken' or 'grief-stricken'. But these once vital words have long since ceased to secrete any freshness of vision. The question 'What do I feel?' is rarely answered by pulling a ready-to-wear word off the shelf.

For now, Ella is lost for words. Neither of us can see clearly. We are both storm-blind. The temptation to grab a lifeboat word out of my own harbour is very strong, but to do so at this moment would risk drowning the emergent truth of her experience. What matters here is Ella's insight, her upwelling truth. We need language which does not merely approximate or label her experience, but which offers us a precise and vital expression. Using the calm of my voice to steady her, I simply repeat Ella's words. 'He's leaving you.' Then we wait.

For what feels like an age, Ella is speechless. She stares at me wide-eyed, with the look of a creature baffled by needless cruelty.

To hold her in these labour pains, I need to have faith in the power of her own articulation. The insight we are seeking is unthought and unspoken. Self-willed. Wild. It will step forward like a deer into a forest clearing, emerging only if we wait patiently, quietly, reverently.

*

At last, from somewhere very far away, Ella says 'I feel… shredded.' The word rips through the space between us in one long, tearing sound of abrasive consonants, 'shhhhhhhrrrrrreded'. Her jaw clenched tight, Ella drags the sound across the space between us like a harrow carving into sods of earth. In the extended 'shr' I hear something tearing apart.

Language like this arrives naked, vital and raw. It delivers 'thought so passionate and alive, that, like the spirit of a plant or an animal, it has an architecture of its own, and adorns nature with a new thing.'[93]

*Shred (v): to tear into shreds something that was once whole*

The word Ella has found to describe her feeling state is not a static noun. It comes from a verb that carries the vital energy of 'losing'. It shows us that her loss is not a past event, a consequence, it is a happening which is still taking place. Her heart is a mangle of conflicted feelings.

Ella's utterance is simple, commonplace, unadorned. Yet in its humble arc it conjures up images that allow us to see into the marrow of her experience. The person she loves has been torn away, leaving her with a rent in the living tissue of her being. This is not a clean cut. She has not been axed with a single honest blow. For months she has fought tooth and nail to save her marriage. The experience has torn her apart. Ella feels dismembered. She is in bits. These bits are not the neatly cut pieces of a jigsaw which can be reassembled, they have been torn across the very grain of her life. Beholding these shreds, she feels irreparably damaged. Ella believes she will never be whole again. It's as though what has been shredded is not only her past life, but also her future self.

Ella needs a new vision. Aware that this new life will seed itself first in the hallowed ground of her imagination, I suggest that she keeps a record of her dreams. For several weeks there is a deafening silence. Ella's sleep is empty. Harrowed and sorrowed, her imaginal ground remains hard, cold and barren. Dumbfounded, she waits. There is nothing she can do but 'stand there, balked and dumb, stuttering and stammering'. The pain of this mute desolation is hard to bear.

Then, one rain-torn morning, Ella arrives at her session with a dream recorded in muffled and sleepy tones onto her phone. 'It's probably nothing,' she says.

> I am leaving home. Moving house. Going somewhere new. I'm surrounded by boxes, each one carefully packed with my belongings. My books, music, clothes. I am gathering my things, packing them ready for the move, but each time I look around, the boxes have been turned upside down, their contents strewn all over the floor. Books are scattered about with pages ripped from them. Clothes lie torn and tattered. It's as though there's an invisible presence lurking behind me, which keeps shredding everything. I feel helpless, useless, stupid. I just can't seem to get it together.

The language of the unconscious is wonderfully precise. It needs a faithful transcription. In Ella's account of her dream, two words in particular leap out. There is the repetition of shredding of course, but there is also the idea of gathering. Beyond its physical meaning of collecting together, 'gathering' means to understand, to comprehend, to see clearly. Something seems to be getting in the way of Ella seeing herself clearly. Without a coherent image, she remains blind. Her life continues to tear apart and she cannot move on.

Exploring the dream, we begin to wonder about the invisible presence that seems intent on disorder and incoherence. I sense the presence of an internal 'shredder'. Shady dream characters often express disavowed parts of ourselves, so I ask Ella, 'Could there be a hidden part in you which prevents you from gathering your things, from getting it together?' Ella bows her head. Her anguish is palpable. 'I couldn't hold the marriage together,' she tells me, 'no matter how hard I tried.' After a pause she adds, 'I just wasn't enough for him.'

This last statement stops me in my tracks. Ella locates the cause of the marriage break-up in her own deficiency. This ravaging self-belief shreds all possibility of an imagined future in which she can 'get it together' – with anyone.

Returning to the precise language of the dream I remark that the shredding presence lurks 'behind' her. To confront it Ella will need to turn around. The dream demands nothing less than a complete metanoia. I suggest that she re-enter the dream and turn to face the invisible presence. I will stay right by her side as she does this. Ella closes her eyes tightly, as though she wants to prevent the dream from spilling out of her inner realm. 'What do you see?' I ask. 'His face,' she says in a voice which strains under the weight of what stands in front of her. 'My husband. He is laughing. His eyes are cold and unfeeling. They tell me I am pathetic.'

Turning around in a dream often helps us to see the obscured aspect, the missing piece, which lies in the blind spot of our feelings (see chapter four). Ella's dream offers up a mirror not only to her loss, but also (critically) to her sense of herself as 'a loser'. Hidden in the marrow of her distress, we have stumbled on the lair of the internal and ever-present 'shredder'. Shame. Shame is the invisible presence that stops her gathering her things, which prevents her from seeing a wholesome future for herself. And this is where Ella's journey of revisioning her life begins. With the disarming of shame.

Ella and I begin to see a way forward. She must hand back the shame that is not hers to bear. Only then can she begin the task of piecing together a life that can move on. Released from the internal shredding, Ella begins to re-collect, to re-member the worthwhile woman she most essentially is. This gathering is a slow and careful process. Bit by bit she begins to 'get it together'.

From the marrow of her desolation Ella begat the word 'shredded'. In her dream word 'gathering', she found a light with which to chart a course across the wild seas of her grief. Commenting on the sense of revelation that comes from this kind of articulate vision, Jungian psychologist James Hillman writes:

> *Then we realise what a miracle it is to find the right words, words that carry soul accurately, where thought, image and feeling interweave. Then we realise that soul can be made on the spot simply through speech.*[94]

*

In his book Landmarks, a powerful meditation on language and landscape, Robert Macfarlane reminds us that 'we see in words'. Words reveal to us the particular nature, character and meaning of experience. They help us to discern through the action of naming. To name is to christen a living thing with words that wrap themselves around it as closely as skin or pelt. Where labels stamp, solidify and seal, a name is swollen and seeded with story.

In Landmarks, Macfarlane laments the falling away of a once rich and vibrant naming of the natural world. His book begins with a list of nature words recently culled from the Oxford Junior

Dictionary, words like acorn, adder, ash, beech and bluebell. This depletion of vocabulary, he argues, leads inexorably to an impoverishment of perception itself. In place of ash, beech, oak, elm and birch, what we are now more likely to see is 'tree'. In place of primrose, cowslip and dandelion we see 'wildflower', or worse still, 'weed'.

What is being lost here is the infinitely varied poetic vernacular that envisions the distinction of each species. Cowslip originates in cu-slyppe meaning 'cow dung'. It tells us about the place in which this tender little flower thrives. Dandelion derives from the French dent-de-lion, literally lion's tooth. Its name describes the coarsely toothed leaves that distinguish it from other yellow flowers.

Seen through this poetic precision of naming, the manifold wonders of nature find purchase in our hearts:

> ... people exploit what they have merely concluded to be of value, but they defend what they love... and to defend what we love we need a particularising language, for we love what we particularly know.[95]

Reflecting on the rich native vocabulary we once employed to articulate our vision of the world around us, Macfarlane argues that the depletion of nature is both actual and imaginal. The loss of biodiversity is verifiable in real terms, but it is also a function of language deficit. As we crowd ourselves into urban spaces, we are losing our ability to name our native wildlife and topography and 'once they go unnamed they go to some degree unseen.'[96] Unseen they become vulnerable to exploitation and neglect.

*

As a traveller in the landscapes of human nature, I believe we are also losing our ability to name (and so to see) the biodiversity of our human ecology of feeling. I too wish to mark the loss of vocabulary through which we are able to see, to discern and distinguish, the intricate particularity of our emotional worlds. Words like *forlorn*, *bereft*, *forsaken*, *despondent* and *melancholy* lie buried under the dead weight of ubiquitous descriptors, most notably 'depression' and 'anxiety'.

Each of these lost words carries in its belly a story seeded with its own vital vision. *Despondent* was originally coined from the Latin *de* meaning 'away' and *spondere*, meaning 'to promise'. The word was most often used in relation to a father's promise to give away his daughter in marriage. This embedded story gives us a poignant sense of a particular kind of loss which, whilst foreseen, is nonetheless hard to bear, because what is being given away is of great and tender worth. *Bereft* originates in the words *be* + *reafian*, meaning to 'rob' or 'plunder'. It carries the sense of something breaking into our lives and stealing away our treasure. We feel desecrated by a pitiless intruder and the appalling sense that we should have checked the lock on the door. Re-storied, the word voices the sense of violation which is so often present in the early stages of sudden loss.

Shorn of a native language of experience once rich in poetic imagery, we increasingly see our emotional lives through muddy mood words like 'fine' and 'OK', or 'down' and 'low'. These bland descriptors give voice to a turbid mix of feelings, thoughts and sensations. Sometimes our feelings register a gloomy hue because particular emotional shades have been painted over, either by the injunctions of others or by our own disavowal. Often the inner murk simply suggests an experience that has not been clearly articulated. Weighed down by these unintelligible stirrings, we struggle to discern nuance and distinction within the crosscurrents of feeling. Blind to the intelligence of our emotions, we find ourselves increasingly at the mercy of what T. S. Eliot calls 'the general mess of imprecision of feeling, Undisciplined squads of emotion.'[97] We no longer see where we are.

Lost for our own words, we turn increasingly to the language of psychology. We are encouraged to see through a vocabulary littered with abstract nouns that solidify, categorise and label human experience. These labels offer us a semblance of discernment. 'Ah that's what I'm feeling,' we say, relieved someone has got a map and compass. In truth we have just exchanged one bland irreducible descriptor for another. Words like these, Silvia Plath warns, become 'dry and riderless'.[98] Held in their cold embrace our feelings risks being stillborn.

In contrast to the poetry of naming which begets life, labelling presses a new-born feeling into a preconceived terminology. The nascent truth is shoehorned into concepts that have been dislocated from the soil of personal truth. Psychological terminology is awash with bucket words that gather up the exquisite complexity and delicacy of the human condition in a single swill. Words like 'depression' and 'anxiety' cast themselves across human experience like giant trawler nets which indiscriminately capture in their mesh a myriad of finely differentiated species of experience.

So many of the words we use today to articulate our emotions arrive preconfigured. Like paint squeezed straight from the tube, they register as a single shade, a homogenous hue. Artists often complain that pre-mixed pigments lack lustre. They appear dull and lifeless. To create luminous colours, painters combine contrasting hues on the palette. The most vital black hues are created by combining all three primary colours – yellows, reds and blues. The resulting blacks are vibrant and take on an infinite palette of subtly articulated hues and tints.

Artist Paul Klee explored the articulation of compound colour in a series of 'square' paintings in which he fractured colour into a myriad of tones and hues. *Ancient Sound, Abstract on Black* reveals a nuanced palette of blacks surfacing into brighter tones. Looking at Klee's painting it strikes me: No two blacks are the same. By the same token I suggest that no two depressions are the same. No two anxieties are the same either. They are not the same because each experience resonates with a particular pallet of emotional colours, shades and tones.

Used carelessly, diagnostic labels risk forming what novelist Jeannette Winterson calls a 'veil of words that filmy or thick hides myself from the moment, you from me.'[99] Through ubiquitous use they become desiccated and opaque, like cataracts. We no longer see through them to the intimate drama unfolding within.

*

Like music, our emotions are polyphonic (from the Greek polys = 'many' + phone = 'voice'). In polyphonic music several independent melodic lines play simultaneously, crossing over one another. Dissonance and harmony interweave through counterpoints of melody and rhythm, to create a richly textured sound capable of communicating the dynamic complexity of human experience.

In recent decades, psychological terminology seems to be taking a step backwards to a kind of 'monophony' characteristic of early medieval plain chant, which consisted of liturgical texts sung in unison, one note at a time. To visualise the complexity of loss, for example, we are now encouraged to see through a linear framework of 'stages of grief' articulated in a static sequence of inert nouns: Shock, Denial, Anger, Bargaining, Depression, Testing, Acceptance. These abstract nouns pin the butterflies of our hearts to the board.

Experiences of loss are messy, unstable and erratic. Opened and tenderised, our emotions take sudden turns in response to the slightest touch. We are for a time at the mercy of enormously complex cross currents of experience. Confronted with a succession of emptied husk words, we can easily loose our bearings.

The impossibility of seeing emotions in sequence is powerfully articulated by Helen Macdonald in her award-winning memoir *H r Hawk*[100] in which she journals the wildness of her grief in wake of her father's death. Helen recalls her efforts to fit her experience of loss into a linear framework:

> *I wanted to taxonomise the process, order it, make it sensible. But there was no sense, and I didn't recognise any of these emotions at all.*

Helen's efforts to fit her experience into stages prove futile. Her frustration erupts:

> *It was the rage of something not fitting; the frustration of trying to put something in a box that is slightly too small. You try moving the shape around in the hope that some angle will make it fit the box. Slowly comes the apprehension that this might not, after all, be possible.*

As long ago as 1975 James Hillman warned that 'in psychiatry words have become schizogenic, themselves a cause and source of mental disease.'[101] Caught in the web of labels our emotions clog together in an undifferentiated hairball of experience that chokes and congests us. Our feelings appear chaotic, unbidden and dangerous. Trapped between the emptied husks of worn-out words and the fossilised language of experts, our rich human topography of experience risks falling out of view. We seem to have arrived at a blandscape of monumental proportions.

*

We are sentient creatures, fundamentally fluid like water. Our emotions are experiences-in-motion, so our language needs to move with them. The vital dynamics of our inner worlds are much more accurately and tenderly perceived through verbs that move and through symbols that clash together. As Jay Griffiths observes, '... all things that represent life at its most vital and wild wiggle.

Words wiggle into metaphor.'[102] These wiggling words are rarely found in diagnostic glossaries or psychology textbooks. They are woven into a vernacular vocabulary that has been seeded in us over generations through our lived relationships to each other and to the natural world.

Robert Macfarlane reminds us that we see 'in webs of words, wefts of words, woods of words.'[103] We see most deeply through metaphors that hold together counterpoints of feelings, thoughts and sensations, without reducing them to a single form. Increasingly, we walk through woods of words with our heads in the clouds, treading resonant language under foot. So much native vision is lost in this careless wandering. The good news is that we do not have to look very far to find these vital words, for buried in our native dialects lie figures of speech rich in symbol. Our everyday language is littered with metaphor.

Sometimes, when we get lost in our sorrow, we stumble on words, or webs of words, which have become dull through neglect. Some lie buried under the mantle of desiccating labels. Others, like the first snowdrops of spring, press through the still-hard ground of our grief. Picking a few of these up, we breathe life into them and so begin to see through to the story that is quickening within us.

*

Ella looks gloomy today. She has not worked since her marriage fell apart nine months ago. Despite numerous job applications she has been unable to progress beyond a first interview. The world seems unkind and pitiless. Her finances are dwindling. 'I just don't seem to be able to get anything off the ground,' she tells me. It's a common enough expression. Easy to overlook. But something in its simple poetic vision makes me stop and wonder.

I ask Ella if an image or a story comes to mind when says she is struggling to 'get anything off the ground'. Searching for a moment, her face brightens as a memory ignites within her. She tells me about a time when her son was still a child. He would take a kite out to fly over the windy common that backed onto their house. For a year or two this was his great joy, a magical ritual of trial and error through which he learned how to sniff into the breeze, to discover its dynamics and direction. To get his kite off the ground.

Intrigued by this vision, I ask Ella what she learned from her son about flying a kite. She explains to me the importance of taking time to set out the kite in just the right orientation to the wind, to hold the string just short enough to create some resistance to the breeze, but gently enough so that it can release as the air begins to take it up. At the end of this account I ask what she understands to be the single most important step. 'It's not so much a step as a sort of conviction,' she replies. I give her a questioning look. 'Yes, the conviction that if you run with all your heart, the wind will do the rest.' Pausing to register this insight she adds, 'If you doubt this for one minute, the kite won't make it off the ground.' Sensing Ella has stumbled on the crux of the matter, I ask 'And do you feel that you are applying for these jobs with all your heart?' She shakes her head. 'No. Not with very much of my heart at all.'

Ella has been going through the motions, tying her actions to an image of herself that has run out of breath. The very thought of returning to the soulless work which has preoccupied her for the last twenty years makes her heart feel heavy with despair. No wonder she can't get anything off the ground.

Ella's despair signifies a loss of hope. Our word 'despair' derives from the French word for hope, *espoir*, which shares its root with the word 'speed' (from the Latin *sperare*). Both words originally evoked the idea of a 'quickening'. Perhaps this quickening is what Ella's son experienced when he ran the kite 'with all his heart'. Hope is a quickening in the heart, an uplift of spirit. The Hebrew word for spirit, *Ruah*, and the Greek *Pneuma*, both originate in the idea of breath, or wind. Pregnant with story, Ella's simple figure of speech encompasses all of this insight. The poetry of her expression has not merely reproduced the visible. It has made the invisible apparent.

Through her simple expression Ella begins to see that she needs to take her creative will to a different place, where the uplift of her desire is authentic and strong. Over the following months, we begin to gather memories, dreams and longings that lift her heart. Sniffing into the breeze, there is a quickening deep within her.

Ella picks up the scent of fresh hope.

*

In an age where the power to name experience is outsourced to experts, we are perhaps losing sight of the searing (seer-ing) truth which sounds within the speech of ordinary people. Increasingly accustomed to grabbing words out of the manual, we have lost faith in the wellspring of language that is conceived within all of us. Perhaps we need to recall, as James Hillman does here, that language was once an instrument of revelation:

> *Words like angels, are powers which have invisible power over us…*
> *Without the inherence of soul in words, speech would not move us,*
> *words would not provide forms for carrying our lives and giving*
> *sense to our deaths.*[104]

Severed from an articulate vision rooted in the poetic vernacular of everyday experience, we find ourselves at the mercy of blind forces that cannot release their truth into action. Clogged up with a tangle of feeling, we are increasingly inclined to numb the part that feels so gloomy. Through our screens and our addictions, we close our senses to the wisdom at the heart of our sorrow.

\*

Seeing is a creative act. Those of us who see deeply, Virginia Woolf suggests, do not merely record life. We bring life into being:

> We are not slaves bound to suffer incessantly unrecorded petty blows on our bent backs. We are not sheep either, following a master. We are creators. We too have made something that will join the innumerable congregations of past time. [105]

Through cultivating a deep and tender vision we can reclaim dimensions of experience rich in new beginnings and personal significance. Seeing through the heart of our sorrow, we discover a realm of human nature full of hidden wonders. Reconnected to our own source of replenishment and renewal, we might begin to cherish, rather than to plunder, the natural world around us.

EPILOGUE

# THE NATURE OF INSIGHT

1.  Insight involves the beholding and discernment of someone in their fullness, distinction and significance.
2.  Seeing deeply transforms both the person seen and the seer.
3.  How we open and when we close defines what and how much we see.
4.  Time is a dimension of seeing.
5.  To see deeply we need to move. Seeing through multiple perspectives allows us to comprehend what we see.
6.  Our seeing of each other needs to be underpinned by a respect for concealment.
7.  We see (and are seen) through our touching. We touch (and are touched) through our seeing.
8.  Therapy is a seeing place. Like theatre, this sealed chamber illuminates the obscure and makes ordinary life more vivid.
9.  Discernment is rooted in the art of subtraction. To capture the decisive detail we must let go of everything else.
10. Darkness sharpens seeing.
11. We see through words.
12. We defend what we love. We love what we particularly know. We particularly know through seeing deeply.

# ABOUT THE AUTHOR

I was born on the shores of Lake Titicaca in the high Altiplano of the Bolivian Andes. My compass has always pointed down, towards hidden valleys, in search of the origins and roots of life. I studied history at Cambridge and later photography at Camberwell College of Arts in London. Through the lens of my faithful Nikon camera, with its manual aperture and shutter settings, I discovered how to see the natural world in all its intricate and infinitely surprising wonder.

My early career took me first into publishing and advertising. Then I worked for a number of years in international development with Save the Children, latterly as their Head of Corporate Fundraising. During this time I witnessed the extraordinary creativity of the human spirit, our capacity to renew and reshape lives buried beneath the rubble of suffering and disaster.

My mid-thirties marked a turning point. I entered a period of soul-searching during which I felt increasingly disenchanted. I had a successful career and everything to be thankful for, but something unbidden and unknown disturbed my peace of mind. A friend's mother suggested psychotherapy. The rest, as they say, is history.

A few years later, following a journey to the Himalayan kingdom of Ladakh, I changed course and trained as a psychotherapist, graduating in 2007 with an MA from the

Institute of Psychosynthesis. Developed a hundred years ago by Italian psychiatrist Roberto Assagioli, a contemporary of Jung, *Psychosynthesis* differs from most other psychological perspectives in proposing that the hidden dimension of our unconscious is not merely the repository of historical wounding, but also the wellspring of all that we may be. Assagioli explored the idea that we are each born with a unique identity and purpose embedded in us (rather like the potential oak tree enfolded within an acorn). At various points in our lives this unique and sovereign identity pushes through our habitual mindsets and historical defences, unsettling our emotions and demanding our attention. Repression of this potential can be every bit as painful and debilitating as the impact of childhood wounding. This perspective on suffering as meaningful has profoundly shaped my practice as a psychotherapist and underpins the journeys of revelation and renewal that I share in this book.

Over the past two decades, my work has centred on private practice with men and women from all walks of life. A passionate educator, I am also a Training Therapist with the Psychosynthesis and Education Trust and a Therapy Supervisor. *Hidden Wonders of the Human Heart* is my first book. During the process of writing it, I set aside all my psychology texts and determined to avoid using the increasingly opaque language of my profession. I hope that by using a more accessible vocabulary I might play a part in opening up a way of speaking about human suffering that is less mired in pathology. It is important to stress that psychological theory has been instrumental in directing my vision, but it has always been the lens through which I look and not the living eye which sees.

*Susan Holliday, April 2021*

# ACKNOWLEDGEMENTS

This book is the fruit of a lifetime's practice of seeing deeply which began with a love of the natural world. I am grateful to my brother Peter, whose sense of wonder and close attention to the details of nature seeded in my childhood the joy of looking.

Every story shared in these pages owes its vision to the insight of the men and women who have explored the heart of their sorrow in my therapy practice. I owe each of them a great debt. The stories presented here are creative collages which allow me to portray hours of perceptive exploration in an accessible form. To preserve the anonymity of the individuals involved, I have modified events and circumstances, and concealed identifying details. I have made every effort to respect confidentiality, while remaining true to the spirit of the work.

In developing my therapy practice, I have been blessed with kind and wise teachers. My thanks go to all my trainers at the Institute of Psychosynthesis in London and to my supervisors who continue to hold me in their sight. Amongst these I would especially like to thank Sue Holland and Keith Silvester.

I wish to thank all those who have helped shape the journey of writing this book. Foremost amongst these are Sonia Lakshman, for inspiration and keeping my feet to the flame, and David Boyle, for his unstinting belief that I might have something original to say. I am immensely grateful to Lucy Jones, Jill Hopper,

Chris Robertson, Deanna Fernie, Ian Tattum, Michael Csanyi-Wills, Nunziatina Del Vecchio, Lella Russo and Patrick Clahar for reading the book at various stages and offering me their appreciation and their critique in equal measure. My thanks also go to Kate Straus, Jennie Meadows and Alice Burnett for their friendship and support.

Thankyou to Dee Nickerson for the ravishing painting which adorns the book's cover, to Sue Lascelles for her editorial insight and to my copyright editor Helen Bartlett for her patient persistence. Thanks also to everyone at Troubador Publishing for the care they have shown during the publishing of this book.

My deepest thanks go to my children Jasper and Oscar whose relentless ribbing and good humour have kept me from taking this project too seriously and to my husband Anthony whose love and support have made the book possible.

*

I would like to thank the following copyright holders for permission to reproduce material:

Excerpt from *The Zen of Seeing: Seeing/Drawing as Meditation* by Frederick Franck, copyright ©1973 by Frederick Franck. Used by permission of Alfred A.Knopf, an imprint of the Knopf Doubleday Publishing Group, a division of Penguin Random House LLC. All rights reserved.

Excerpts from Albert Einstein's *Essay to Leo Baeck, 23 February 1953, AEA 35-14* and from his *Letter to Heinrich Zangger, 10 March 1914, regarding his work on the general theory of relativity. CPAE, Vol.5, Doc 513, AEA 39-661,* copyright © The Hebrew University of Jerusalem. With permission of the Albert Einstein Archives.

As the author I have made every effort to obtain permission to reproduce copyright material throughout this book. If any proper acknowledgement has not been made, or permission not received, I would invite the copyright holder to make me aware of this oversight.

# SOURCES

1   Franck, Frederick, *The Zen of Seeing* (Random House, 1973).

AUTHOR'S NOTE

2   Rainer Maria Rilke, *Letters to a Young Poet*, VIII, August 12, 1904.
3   Ibid.
4·  Ibid.
5   Alexander Gilchrist, 'Life of William Blake' in *Gilchrist on Blake*, ed. by Richard Holmes (Harper Perennial, 2005).
6   Martha Graham, 'An Athlete of God' in *This I Believe: The Personal Philosophies of Remarkable Men and Women*, ed. by Jay Allison and Dan Gediman (Holt Paperback, 2007).
7   Vincent Van Gogh, 'Letter to his brother Theo, 3 September 1888' in *The Letters of Vincent van Gogh*, ed. by Ronald de Leeuw (Penguin Books, 1997).

INTRODUCTION

8   Albert Einstein, 'Essay to Leo Baeck, 23 February 1953' (The Albert Einstein Archives).
9   Albert Einstein, 'Letter to Heinrich Zangger, 10 March 1914' (The Albert Einstein Archives).
10  *Antidepressant Drugs Market: Industry Trends, Share, Size, Top Key*

*Players and Forecast Research 2020–2025* (Brand Essence Market Research, January 2020).

CHAPTER ONE

11    George Eliot, *Middlemarch* (Penguin Classics, 1994), Ch.20.

12    Emmanuel Levinas, *Totality and Infinity. An Essay on Exteriority* (Duquesne University Press, 1969).

13    Ibid.

14    Emmanuel Levinas, *Ethics and Infinity: Conversations with Philippe Nemo* (Duquesne University Press, 1985).

15    Agnes De Mille, *Martha: The Life and Work of Martha Graham* (Vintage, 1992).

16    Hermann Hesse, *Beneath the Wheel* (Macmillan USA, Reprint edition, 2005).

17    John G. Neihardt, *Black Elk Speaks: The Complete Edition* (Bison Books, 2014).

18    George Eliot, *Middlemarch* (Penguin Classics, 1994), Ch.20.

19    Jung, C. G. *Modern Man in Search of a Soul* (Kegan Paul, 1933).

20    Bill Brandt, *Camera in London* (Focal, 1948), p.14.

21    Sigmund Freud, *The Future of an Illusion* (W. W. Norton, 1961), p.10.

22    Ibid, p.15.

23    Jay Griffiths, *Wild: An Elemental Journey* (Penguin Books, 2008), p.162.

24    C. G. Jung, *Dream Analysis: Notes on a lecture given in 1928–1930* (Routledge & Kegan Paul, 1984), p.142.

25    Jeannette Winterson, *Art Objects* (Vintage Books, 1996), p.151.

26    Iain McGilchrist, *The Master and his Emissary: The Divided Brain and the Making of the Western World* (Yale University Press, 2010), p.5.

CHAPTER TWO

27    Bill Brandt, *Camera in London* (Focal, 1948), p.14.

28 Nan Shepherd, *The Living Mountain* (Canongate Books, 2011), p.106.

29 Frederick Franck, *The Zen of Seeing* (Random House, 1973).

30 Paul Cézanne, *Conversations with Cézanne*, ed. by Michael Doran (University of California Press, 2001), p.136

31 The Bible: Hebrews 11:1

32 Kathleen Raine, 'Scala Coeli', 1964, in *The Collected Poems of Kathleen Raine* (Golgonooza Press, 2008).

33 T. S. Eliot, 'East Coker', 1944, *Four Quartets* (Faber and Faber, 2001).

34 The Bible: Luke 2:10.

35 Rose-Lynn Fisher, *The Topography of Tears* (Bellevue Literary Press, 2017).

36 Master Sung Tung Po, eleventh century poet and painter.

37 Miles Davis, jazz musician, 1926–1991.

## CHAPTER THREE

38 Stanley Kunitz, '*The Wild Braid*': *A Poet reflects on a Century in the Garden* (W. W. Norton & Co, 2007).

39 Paul Cézanne, *Conversations with Cézanne*, ed. by Michael Doran (University of California Press, 2001).

40 C. G. Jung, *The Psychology of the Transference*, CW 16, par. 492 (Routledge, 1998), p.119.

41 James Hillman, *Revisioning Psychology* (Harper Perennial, 1992), p.121

## CHAPTER FOUR

42 Mark Twain, *Following the Equator* (American Publishing Co and Doubleday & McLure Co, 1987), p.654.

43 T. S. Eliot, 'Little Gidding', 1942, *Four Quartets* (Faber and Faber, 2001).

44 Christopher Bollas, *The Shadow of the Object: Psychoanalysis of the Unthought Known* (Routledge, 1987).

45 Victor Hugo, *Post-scriptum de ma vie* (Calmann Levy, 1901), p.90.

46  Kirsten H. Peterson and Anna Rutherford, *Chinua Achebe: A Celebration* (Heinemann, 1991).

47  Elaine Aron, *The Highly Sensitive Person* (Harper Collins, 2017).

CHAPTER FIVE

48  Kathleen Raine, 'The Instrument', in *Selected Poems* (Golgonooza Press, 1988).

49  Russell Freedman, *Martha Graham: A Dancer's Life* (Houghton Mifflin, 1998), p.12.

50  Agnes De Mille, *Martha: The Life and Work of Martha Graham* (Vintage Books, 1992).

51  Etheridge Knight, *On the Oral Nature of Poetry*, a talk given at Colorado State University on 8 February 1987, as a guest of the Fina Arts Series.

52  Agnes De Mille, *Martha: The Life and Work of Martha Graham* (Vintage Books, 1992).

53  Stanley Kunitz, *'The Wild Braid': A Poet Reflects on a Century in the Garden* (W. W. Norton & Co, 2007).

54  Stanley Kunitz, 'The Snakes of September' from *The Collected Poems* (W. W. Norton & Co, 1985).

55  Lawrence Anthony, with Graham Spence, *The Elephant Whisperer* (Sidgwick and Jackson, 2009).

56  Ibid, p.86.

57  Françoise Anthony, 'Trust is earned', a television commercial for Coronation Fund Managers.

58  Barbara Hepworth, *A Pictorial Autobiography* (Praeger Publishers, NY, 1971).

59  Paul Cézanne, 'The Three Dialogues of Joachim Gasquet' in *Conversations with Cezanne*, ed. by Michael Doran (University of California Press, 2001).

60  Stanley Kunitz, *'The Wild Braid': A Poet Reflects on a Century in the Garden* (W. W. Norton & Co, 2007).

CHAPTER SIX

61 Sanford Meisner and Dennis Longwell, *Sanford Meisner On Acting* (Vintage, 1987).

62 Brené Brown, *Daring Greatly: How the courage to be vulnerable transforms the way we live, love, parent and lead* (Penguin, 2015).

63 Stanley Kunitz, 'The Wild Braid': *A Poet Reflects on a Century in the Garden* (W. W. Norton & Co, 2007).

64 Konstantin Stanislavski, *An Actor Prepares* (Bloomsbury Academic, 2013), p.72.

65 Ibid, p.71.

66 Ibid, p.72.

67 Leonardo da Vinci, *Delphi Complete Works of Leonardo da Vinci* (Delphi Classics, 2014), p.1150.

CHAPTER SEVEN

68 Arvo Pärt, 'An Interview with Arvo Pärt, Sources of Invention', Geoff Smith (*The Musical Times*, 1999).

69 Arvo Pärt, *Liner notes for Fratres*, 1977.

70 Daniel Barenboim, *The Phenomenon of Sound* in 'The Barenboim Journal'.

71 Konstantin Stanislavski, *An Actor Prepares* (Bloomsbury Academic, 2013), p.151.

72 Sanford Meisner, *Sanford Meisner On Acting* (Vintage, 1987), p.34.

73 Bill Evans, Liner notes to Miles Davis album 'Kind of Blue', 1959.

74 Virginia Woolf, *Collected Essays, Vol. IV, 1925-1928*, ed. by A. McNeillie (Harvest Books, 2008).

75 Virginia Woolf, *To the Lighthouse* (The Hogarth Press, 1927).

76 Rainer Maria Rilke, *Letters to a Young Poet*, II, August, 1904.

77 Henri Cartier-Bresson, Fondation Henri Cartier-Bresson.

78 Henri Cartier-Bresson, *The Decisive Moment* (Simon and Schuster, 1952).

79    Henri Cartier-Bresson, 'Interview with Richard Avedon', 2000, (https://www.youtube.com/watch?v=aKBSkNuUqAc)

80    Henri Cartier-Bresson, *The Decisive Moment* (Simon and Schuster, 1952).

81    Meister Eckart, *The Complete Mystical Works of Meister Eckart* (Crossroad Publishing Company, 2009).

CHAPTER EIGHT

82    Stanley Kunitz, *'The Wild Braid': A Poet Reflects on a Century in the Garden* (W. W. Norton & Co, 2007).

83    C. S. Lewis, *The Lion, the Witch and the Wardrobe* (Geoffrey Bles, 1950), p.4.

84    Ibid, p.5.

85    John Keats, 'Letter to George and Thomas Keats, 22 December 1818'.

86    Barry Lopez, *Threshold* (Granta 140, Summer 2017).

87    James S. Grotstein, *A Beam of Intense Darkness: Wilfred Bion's Legacy to Psychoanalysis* (Karnac Books, 2007), p.1.

CHAPTER NINE

88    John Ruskin, *Modern Painters Vol 3, Part IV, Chapter XVI*, 1856, p.333.

89    Marcel Proust, in *Upheavals of Thought* by Martha C. Nussbaum (Cambridge University Press, 2001).

90    T. S. Eliot, 'East Coker', 1944, *Four Quartets* (Faber and Faber, 2001).

91    Matsuo Basho, from the introduction to *The Narrow Road to the Deep North*, trans. Nobuyuki Yuasa (Penguin Books, Harmondsworth, 1966), p.33.

92    Ralph Waldo Emerson, 1844, *The Poet* (Create Space, 2017), p.37.

93    Ibid, p.14.

94    James Hillman, *The Essential James Hillman: A Blue Fire*, ed. by Thomas Moore (Routledge, 1989), p.29.

95   Wendell Berry, *Life is a Miracle: An Essay Against Modern Superstition* (Counterpoint, 2000), p.41.

96   Robert Macfarlane, *Landmarks* (Penguin, 2015).

97   T. S. Eliot, 'East Coker', 1944, *Four Quartets* (Faber and Faber, 2001).

98   Sylvia Plath, 'Words' in *Collected Poems* (Faber and Faber, 1981).

99   Jeanette Winterson, *Art Objects* (Vintage, 1996).

100  Helen Macdonald, *H is for Hawk* (Vintage, 2014), pp.16–17, 141

101  James Hillman, *The Essential James Hillman, A Blue Fire*, ed. by Thomas Moore (Routledge, 1989), p.28.

102  Jay Griffiths, *Wild: An Elemental Journey* (Penguin, 2006).

103  Robert Macfarlane, *Landmarks* (Penguin, 2015).

104  James Hillman, *Revisioning Psychology* (Harper Perennial, 1992), p.9.

105  Virginia Woolf, 'The Waves', 1931, in *The Selected Works of Virginia Woolf* (Wordsworth, 2012).

**Matador**